Just in Case!!

Lose Your Heart, Not Your Mind: The Smart Woman's Guide to Marriage and Self-Sufficiency

Brick Tower Press
Habent Sua Fata Libelli

Just in Case!!

Lose Your Heart, Not Your Mind: The Smart Woman's Guide to Marriage and Self-Sufficiency

By Aliette H. Carolan, Esq.

Brick Tower Press
Habent Sua Fata Libelli

Brick Tower Press
Manhanset House
Dering Harbor, New York 11965

bricktower@aol.com • www.BrickTowerPress.com

Library of Congress Cataloging-in-Publication Data

Carolan, Aliette H.
Just In Case!! Lose Your Heart, Not Your Mind: The Smart Woman's Guide to
Marriage and Self-Sufficiency
p. cm.

1. Law : Family Law - Divorce & Separation. 2. Family & Relationships :
Divorce & Separation
Non-fiction, I. Title.

ISBN: 978-1-899694-73-0, Hardcover

Copyright © 2017 by Aliette H. Carolan

Table of Contents

Biography

In a legal career spanning more than a decade, Aliette H. Carolan, Esq., an *AV Rated-Preeminent* Complex Marital & Family Law attorney, has handled hundreds of divorce cases in Miami, Florida, a city that ranks among the top ten in the U.S. for highest divorce rate. After gaining valuable experience from some of the best family law practitioners in Miami-Dade County, she established her own firm in 2009. Today, her legal team handles high-end, complex family and matrimonial law and reproductive law cases in several counties throughout Florida.

Her high success rate as a *Florida Supreme Court Certified Family Law Mediator* demonstrates her skill at settling complex marital and family law disputes in pre-suit mediation and initial and/or post judgment actions. Her philosophy is that mediation is the best initial course of action, as all parties benefit from first attempting to resolve matters amicably prior to engaging in both financially and emotionally taxing litigation. If mediation does not succeed then she will thoroughly prepare and passionately utilize her honed trial skills to successfully resolve a case.

She was named as a Rising Star in 2014 and a Super Lawyer in 2015 and 2016, by Super Lawyers, a peer review rating service that includes only 2.5% and 5% respectively of outstanding attorneys who have attained a high-degree of peer recognition and professional achievement in Florida. She achieved a Superb Attorney rating by Avvo, also based on peer and client reviews. She is named Top 40 under 40 by the The National Advocates and a Lifetime Member of the Worldwide Who's Who registry of Executives, Professionals and Entrepreneurs. She sits on the Young Collector's Council for the Perez Art Museum Miami and on the Board of Directors of Beaux Arts – Lowe Art Museum, University of Miami.

She is a frequent guest on news shows on CNN in Espanol, PBS, Telemundo, and Univision where she provides expert insight on family law matters such as child custody issues, divorce, child abductions and surrogacy matters. She has also been published and/or cited in several professional journals.

Ms. Carolan earned her J.D. from Nova Southeastern University in 2003 and her B.S. at the University of Miami 1999. She studied International and Comparative Law at the Paris Institute, in Paris, France and attended the Foreign Policy Seminar at American University in Washington, D.C.

She is a member of the Florida Bar (Family Law Section); the United States District Court, Southern District of Florida; the American Bar Association (Family Law Section and Reproductive Section) and the First Family Law Inns of Court.

Acknowledgments

Alan Morell – my brilliant agent - for having a vision for this book, your guidance, humor and support throughout this process.

John Colby – my publisher – for believing in this idea.

Ann Voorhees Baker, Esq. – for your mentorship, your wisdom and insights throughout the writing of this book.

David – for your unwavering support of my ambitions.

Armando E. Hernandez-Rey, MD – for always believing in me and for inspiring me by your example and will to succeed.

Irma y Armando - se lo debo todo a ustedes.

Francesca & Veronica – everything I do, is with you in mind. You are my greatest teachers. I love you with all my heart.

Introduction

You're a smart woman, right? You know a good deal when you see one, and you also know when you're being taken for a ride. Whether you're shopping at a store or ordering at a restaurant, if you're offered something that looks too good to be true, a red flag goes up and you proceed with caution. Most of us would like to think of ourselves as that savvy, self-aware woman who's not easily fooled, who knows what she's getting into each time.

So why does this common sense evaporate right out of our heads when it comes to love and marriage? When the prince rides up on his white horse and gets down on one knee, why does the practical, careful, analytical side of us zonk out like Sleeping Beauty under the spell of the bad fairy's curse? Who even believes in these storybook clichés?

The answer is a fair number of us, if you consider divorce statistics and the financial outcomes of women who've put marriage, spouse and family above all else. The American myth of "marry for love, devote yourself to your husband and children, and you'll live happily ever after" is failing hundreds of thousands of women every year. According to a 2011 Census Bureau report, in 2009 women who divorced in the previous 12 months were twice as likely as recently divorced men to be in poverty.[1] Writer and essayist Laura Lillibridge notes, "The word contract is used to describe both marriage and business, with one big difference; we go into marriage with a naïve, 'YES! Whatever, forever! Love conquers all!'" Married twice, Lillibridge admits to being the instigator of divorce in both situations. She says, "There's an old adage, 'Men marry women hoping that they will never change, but women marry men hoping to change them,' and in many cases I think this is true"; yet she acknowledges that neither view is entirely correct.[2]

Lillibridge herself isn't entirely correct. Marriage is a contract, but it's also a deal we make with our hearts when we should be evaluating what we're entering into with our heads. Long before you say "I do," and even before you say "yes" to someone on bended knee, you have to know the deal you are making. Whether you acknowledge it or not, you're giving up freedom, self-determination and self-sufficiency if you view marriage as a safety net absolving you from any further need to be accountable for - and responsible to - yourself. The potential mate who sails in to save the day isn't saving you from anything if you abdicate everything to him and say to yourself, "No worries. He's going to take care of everything from now on."

As a family law and divorce attorney who's argued hundreds of cases, I can say with absolute certainty that the wife who is oblivious to her husband's income and expenditures, family finances, bank and credit accounts, loans and other fiscal matters is the wife who finds herself struggling to stay afloat in the aftermath of divorce. When push comes to shove, the only person he's going to take care of is himself, and if you haven't maintained your own savings account, ensured yourself a steady income source whether it's earnings or investments, and established your own credit, you haven't taken care of yourself to the best of your ability. And if you haven't taken care of yourself, once the dust of divorce settles, you'll have little to show for your love, devotion and dedication to him and the kids.

Give away your heart, but don't lose your mind. Know the deal you're getting into. Know that self-preservation is the key to a happy marriage - and a happy divorce. We don't take a job expecting that we'll hate it and quit. We don't sign the lease on an apartment thinking we'll be sick of it in six months, and we don't enter into a relationship planning for the breakup. But the flip side is that we shouldn't expect that any relationship we enter into will save us from the responsibility of being self-sufficient. No matter where you are in the process - dating, engaged, married, or contemplating separation and divorce - if you can realize why you have to put yourself first, you're halfway there. Whether you're in the rapturous throes of endless love or the first moments of stomach-churning awareness that your marriage is falling apart, this book is for you. It's for every woman who understands that self-preservation will not happen if you rely on someone else to save you. You need to maintain - or begin to establish - your personal independence and financial solvency if you want to be self-sufficient no matter what life throws at you. You can lean on someone, but you have to be able to stand on your own two feet at a moment's notice, and that's what this book is about.

I can take you through what you need to do, step by step, to assure your own secure future. It's never too early, although it can be too late if you wait too long. I speak from personal experience and from the experiences of the many women I've helped as they sought to end their marriages and come out with the best deal possible in the wake of their divorces. You'll hear some of their stories in the pages ahead. My approach isn't emotional, biased, or vindictive; those approaches fail. Instead I advocate the use of reason and logic. The advice I'm sharing is what I'd give my best friend to spare her heartache and regret. Follow it and chances are you won't experience it either. Because in the end, the only person you can completely rely on is yourself.

Research:

1. Elliott, Diana B. and Tavia Simmons, "Marital Events of Americans: 2009 - American Community Survey Reports," United States Census Bureau, U.S. Department of Commerce Economics and Statistics Administration, August 2011. http://www.census.gov/prod/2011pubs/acs-13.pdf

2. Lillibridge, Laura, "What If We Treated Marriage More Like the Contract It Is?" *Huffpost Divorce*, *The Huffington Post*, November 27, 2013. http://www.huffingtonpost.com/lara-lillibridge/marriage-contract_b_4351772.html?

Checklist of the Signs That Your Marriage is Heading for Divorce

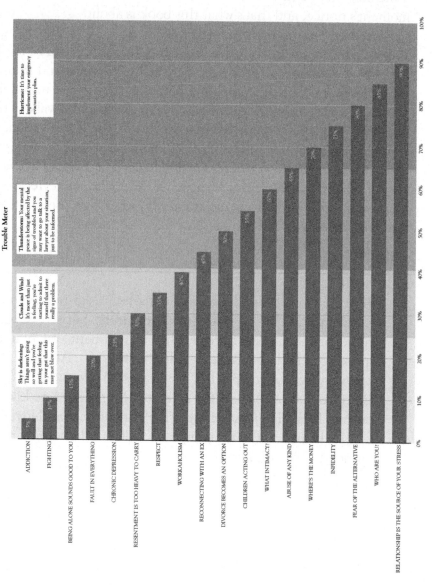

Trouble Meter

Sky is darkening: Things aren't going so well and you're getting that feeling in your gut that this may not blow over.

Clouds and Wind: It's more than just a feeling, you're starting to admit to yourself that there really a problem.

Thunderstorm: Your mental peace is being affected by the signs of trouble and you may want to go talk to a lawyer about your situation, just to be informed.

Hurricane: It's time to implement your emergency evacuation plan.

- ADDICTION — 5%
- FIGHTING — 10%
- BEING ALONE SOUNDS GOOD TO YOU — 15%
- FAULT IN EVERYTHING — 20%
- CHRONIC DEPRESSION — 25%
- RESENTMENT IS TOO HEAVY TO CARRY — 30%
- RESPECT — 35%
- WORKAHOLISM — 40%
- RECONNECTING WITH AN EX — 45%
- DIVORCE BECOMES AN OPTION — 50%
- CHILDREN ACTING OUT — 55%
- WHAT INTIMACY? — 60%
- ABUSE OF ANY KIND — 65%
- WHERE'S THE MONEY — 70%
- INFIDELITY — 75%
- FEAR OF THE ALTERNATIVE — 80%
- WHO ARE YOU? — 85%
- RELATIONSHIP IS THE SOURCE OF YOUR STRESS — 90%

PART ONE

What To Do Before
"I Do" - Engagement - Prenup

Chapter 1

What a Girl Wants

You've found the person you want to spend the rest of your life with, and you've either gotten engaged or you're about to say yes. You seem happy, and if that's really the case, congratulations - that's wonderful news. But let's back up a bit before we pop the champagne cork and start pouring. Why do you want to get married? Not to this person specifically, but to anyone? What is your vision of marriage, and what is it based on? What do want out of marriage, and what do you expect from it? When we buy a house, we work with a realtor who typically asks, "What's on your must-have list? Number of bedrooms, bathrooms? Backyard, garage, attic, basement? Good schools, proximity to public transportation, trees and landscaping or a low maintenance exterior? Do you want move-in ready or are you willing to look at a fixer upper?" These questions are essential to every successful house hunt, and they're the backbone of countless cable TV shows. The more potential homeowners tick off their lists, the more likely they are to make an offer and end up with their dream home. If it works for buying a house, it should work for choosing a spouse, right? So where's your checklist of must-haves, negotiables, if-possibles and deal breakers? What do you want in a long-term partner, and is the person you've chosen compatible with your values, your expectations, and the life you want to lead? Before you pick a date for your wedding, you need to seriously evaluate everything up to this point. This will require you to take a long, hard look at yourself. Not in front of a mirror, but in a quiet hour of introspection, sitting down with yourself and being completely honest and open about everything in your past and present. If you do the hard work of self-examination now, you will be in a better place to evaluate your future.

Know Yourself

Every one of us is a product of our circumstances and our upbringing, but we do not have be limited by either. You may think you know who you are and what you want, but if ever there was a time in your life in which you need to understand yourself, this is it. Before you make what you intend will be a lasting commitment to another person, it's essential to commit to yourself - your most deeply-held hopes and aspirations, not just what other people expect of you. Now's the time to do the important work of self-evaluation and self-awareness. Give yourself plenty of breathing room to do the following exercise - at least 2-3 hours in a space where you'll have privacy and you won't be interrupted. Take along a notebook to write your answers down, or dictate into your smartphone, tablet or computer. This is a conversation you'll be having with yourself, and it may be one of the most critical moments of your life. Why? Because this is where you'll open up to your most authentic feelings. No judgment, no shaming, just honesty. Go with what arises inside you, and don't censor any of your thoughts. This is where the hard work of relationship begins: With yourself. Ready? Let's begin.

Your Personal History

Sit quietly with yourself and meditate on who you are, what you value and the type of life that you envision for yourself.

- What was your childhood like?
- In terms of birth order, where are you in the family dynamic? What role did you play in your family?
- Are your parents still married or are they divorced? What are you feeling about their marriage?
- What was your socio-economic background?
- Comfortable? Well off? Wealthy? Or were there plenty of financial struggles?
- Did both your parents work, or did one stay at home?
- What did you dream about being when you "grew up"?

I'm going to assume that if you had a stay-at-home parent, it was your mother, since that was and may still be far more common than the opposite situation.

- Did her happiness or unhappiness influence you during your childhood or teenage years?
- Are you aware of her feelings about her choices and decisions?
- Do you think that because your mother stayed home and possibly abandoned her career for you that you have to do the same for your children?
- Do you believe that women who work are not good parents, or not as good as mother's who don't work?
- Do you think that children should be the center of a woman's life while the husband or father should be the sole provider?
- Do you believe that the role of the mother is more important than the role of the father?

To Work or Not to Work

I make no judgments about the decision to work or not work because this is a personal decision that every woman must make for herself.

I believe that our choices in this area are informed by the women who raised us and by our feelings about the subject. Again, who we are is largely dependent on what we know, and so much of our knowledge comes from what we have experienced. Sometimes we set our agendas to obtain what we wish we had when we were younger. In other words, the lives we want either reflect our past or compensate for it. You are working or have worked before marriage, but you may not want to afterwards. What are the reasons that shape this decision?

- Do you think you'll be happier working?
- Not working? Working part-time?
- Working only until you have children?

You may have had strong feelings about the working/not working issue long before you met your potential mate. Although some people are willing to make significant sacrifices to stay at home, it's growing increasingly harder for couples and families to make it on one income alone, unless one partner is extremely successful at his or her career. Perhaps you have professional goals that are important to you or you simply do not have the temperament to stay home with children. Both views are valid and neither position is "better" than the other. I would only caution you by expressing that not working can lead to powerlessness in certain situations, so you have to be mindful of your circumstances during the course of your relationship.

Living the Life

Have you asked yourself what level of lifestyle you will require? Success is predicated on hard work; and if you marry someone who's built a successful career staying at the office until 8 pm every night, and going back in at 6 am the next morning, that lifestyle isn't likely to change. You'll have the material luxuries that most people dream of, but you won't have the kind of spouse who is constantly at your side if you marry someone like this. He may be devoted to you while he's at home, but home won't be a priority, and you're not going to change that. And this may be acceptable to you, as it is with many women. Some women don't mind being responsible for the daily morning and afternoon routines as long as they don't have to be financially responsible for anything. Others prefer to have control of their financial world even if that means less time with the children. These are very personal decisions that must be made by the individual person. What you decide is what you'll have to live with. Go with your gut—there is no wrong or right. Things to consider as you make this decision:

- What neighborhood do you want to live in and what is the price point there?
- Are you going to be happy in a house that just meets your needs or are you going to want to have a more lavish home?
- Are you a Target woman or a Neiman Marcus woman?
- Will you want to provide your children with options for their education, such as private schools, or will you be satisfied with your local public or magnet schools?

Do your homework and investigate what the average annual cost of tuition is in your ideal neighborhood. Figure out how much you spend on grooming, clothes and shoes on an annual basis. Think about the vacations you want to take – will you travel for spring break, and summer and winter break? Are you ok with staying at a Holiday Inn or do you require a posh hotel with amenities?

Money Matters

These questions may sound trivial, but they will factor into the financial circumstances you will need to create, whether through your own efforts combined with your future mate's, or through your husband's efforts alone if you expect he'll be able to provide everything with just his earnings. The bottom line is you have to be honest with yourself and be true to yourself or there's a likelihood that your marriage will fail. Money may not be at the root of all evil, but it has an enormous effect on marriage and is a contributing factor in marriages that fall apart. Cathy Meyer, a Certified Divorce Coach, marriage educator, legal investigator, and Divorce Support Expert at About.com, came up with the top ten causes of marital discord. Money problems lead them all. "Most couples argue over bills, debt, spending, and other financial issues," she says. "How you decide to deal with money problems in your marriage will determine whether those problems have a negative or positive effect on your marriage."

Research:

1. Judging from the advice available at *AskMen.com*, men have the same feelings about money as women do. According to dating and relationship expert Andrew Scott, "Money may be the thing married couples fight about the most. The biggest solution to money problems is to talk about them. Be forthright and honest about things like your debt and adopt a policy of transparency," he advises.

2. Sonya Britt, a Kansas State University researcher, authored the 2012 study, "Examining the Relationship Between Financial Issues and Divorce" published in the journal Family Relations. Drawn from data involving more than 4,500 couples as part of the National Survey of Families and Households, her findings echo the assertion that arguing about money is "the top predictor of divorce." These types of arguments, Britt noted, go on for much longer and are usually more heated than other fights couples engage in: "You can measure people's money arguments when they are very first married. It doesn't matter how long ago it was, but when they were first together and already arguing about money, there is a good chance they are going to have poor relationship satisfaction." She also discovered that relationship satisfaction

drops the longer a couple fights about finances. Her advice to new couples includes premarital counseling with a financial planner, examining each other's credit reports and talking frankly about how both partners will handle money in a way that's fair for both parties. The study's co-author Jeffrey Dew speculates there's more behind the argument than financial concerns. "It may be that fights about money are actually fights about deeper issues in the relationship - power, trust, etc. If these deep issues in the relationship are problematic, then these couples may be more likely to divorce."

3. Meyers, Cathy, "Top 10 Causes of Marital Discord," http://divorcesupport.about.com/od/isdivorcethesolution/qt/marital_discord.htm

4. Moore, Andrew, "Top 10 Causes of Marital Discord," http://www.askmen.com/top_10/dating/top-10-marital-problems_2.html Jacques, Stephanie, "Researcher finds correlation between financial arguments, decreased relationship satisfaction," Kansas State University news release, July 12, 2013. http://www.k-state.edu/media/newsreleases/jul13/predictingdivorce71113.html

5. "Divorce Study: Financial Arguments Early in Relationship Predict Divorce," *Huffpost Divorce*, *The Huffington Post*, July 16, 2013. http://www.huffingtonpost.com/2013/07/12/divorce-study_n_3587811.html

Chapter 2

Just In Case

Now that you've done an honest self-assessment and clearly thought through what it is that you really want for your future – with or without marriage – it's time to take that picture of the ideal future and mold it into a realistic list of wishes and needs with regard to the man you plan to marry. We've all heard of the girl who was the most beautiful girl in the class, the one who always had a boyfriend, the one who is in the best shape yet now she is alone. Some girls seem to be attracting all kinds of men yet they aren't searching consciously; they're actually sitting around waiting for the prince to arrive and it's sad to say that the prince isn't coming.

The Prince Lives Only in a Fairy Tale

The reality is that the fantasy of the prince coming to take you off to live a fantasy life is exactly that – a fantasy. And as appealing as a fantasy is, it is much healthier to temper your expectations and face the reality of who you are and whom your mate in life will actually be like. Your life is what you make of it and you can live the life of your wildest dreams if you take responsibility for it.

There are many men out there who are wonderful husbands, great fathers and true partners. The goal should be to find one of them and not end up with one who you believed, based on your faulty perception rather than empirical evidence, would give you a fantasy life you somehow came to believe you deserve.

Who Is This Man Really?

Just as in Chapter 1, when I asked you to consider certain questions about yourself, I am going to ask you to do the same with regard to your desired companion. The following are just some basic points to consider:

- Does he need to have the same religion as you?
- Does he need to come from the same or higher socioeconomic background?
- Does he share your culture?
- Does his educational background matter to you?
- Would you be OK if he is a tradesman, or do you prefer a professional?
- Does it matter to you if he is in a lucrative field where his income will generally increase annually or is it all right with you if his income plateaus so you'll have to live on a budget (particularly if you will not also work)?
- Is it important to you that he be driven to succeed?
- Do you want him to be the type who has lots of friends and social commitments or do you prefer more of a loner?
- Do you want a man who is an involved father?
- Do you want a man who has strong opinions or do you prefer more of a wallflower?
- Does he have to share your interests or do you prefer to live independent lives?

When you are reviewing your feelings on this subject, try to not think about where you are right now, but project a few years into your life. Change the paradigms around a bit. Try to picture yourself with a kid or two and then rethink your list. Life is like a puzzle not pieced together yet, and the decisions you make in selecting a mate will greatly affect the picture of your life that you will create.

Seek Out Wise Counsel. I encourage you to consider your current needs but also to anticipate your *future* needs. This is hard because there is no replacement for experience, but talking to women who have been there, done that and are willing to share is a great place to start.

I have heard people say, "Make your list, like the 10 commandments, and if he has 7 or 8 of them, give him a shot." The reality is that no one is perfect and life is a series of trade-offs. This is not to meant to suggest you should "settle" or give up on anything you're not sure you can have, but rather that you might want to refine your wants a bit in light of what you know to be within the realm of possibility. It can be very helpful to first make your list, and then back away from it for the moment, and turn to an examination of your overarching values.

Does This Man Fit Your Values?

Are your values centered around: Doing good in the world? Having lots of money? Self-reliance? Being supportive of others? Being financially taken care of as you take care of home and family? At this point, the work you completed in Chapter 1 will come in handy. If you have taken a thorough inventory of yourself, you can come to a place of acceptance of who you truly are and be able to be authentic in your choice of a partner.

Also, once you have gone through the self-evaluation process for yourself, it will be easier to see people for who they really are. Many times, women see their partners as whom they wish them to be and when the reality of who they actually are hits - it drops like a bomb. You will need to have a true understanding of your partner's values before you can determine if they align with yours.

I've learned over the years that aligning values does not always mean having the same values. In a relationship there should be an ebb and flow of energy and a synergy so that the balance of life can be found – or at least aimed for. For example, two very highly competitive, driven people may not be compatible at all. Even though it may feel like they would be, in practice there might not be enough space in the house for all the powerful energy. Although it will require acceptance and patience, there can be strength in the differences between them so that together the union is powerful.

Evaluate Him Without the Romantic Outlook

Once you have found a partner, evaluate him in a very practical, nonjudgmental way. And yes, I realize how not romantic that sounds, but you know what is *really* non-romantic? Divorce with two children and a mountain of debt. I didn't grow up hearing old American adages in my Cuban-American home, so sometimes I confuse them and my husband loves to mock me for it, but I know there's much wisdom in the one about an ounce of prevention saving a pound of grief. It's so true.

So the point is to think clearly about your partner's characteristics, abilities, shortfalls, values, and his vision of an ideal life. Please look past his sex appeal. No matter how attracted you are to him on a physical plane, that will diminish and should never be the basis of forming a true relationship. Finances should also not be the basis for the relationship either if the goal is a true partnership.

Examine your own honest impressions. You have a gut instinct about this person; trust it. And I am not the first person to say this, and I won't be the last, but you are not going to change anyone or improve him or her, or fix him or her. You may be able to carry them along with you for a while, you may be able to make them dress the part you want them to play, but if what you're trying to make of them is not truly who they are when you marry them, you are not going to implant any particular way of being or change their personality, their character, their drive, or any other of their most basic and ingrained traits.

When thinking about the person you have or the person you're looking for, think about specifics, such as:

- Is he a planner or is he impulsive?
- Is he transparent about his income, expenses, and spending, or secretive and dismissive of your questions and concerns?
- How long have you known him, and how *well* do you know him?
- Does he have friends, and do you like them? Or is he a bit of a loner?
- How does he get along with his own family?
- Do your friends and family members like him?
- Who's the one with the bigger income, and does this affect where the power lies in the relationship?
- Does he talk about his future and his professional goals – and does he *have* professional goals?
- Is he religious and you are not, or vice-versa? If both of you are religious, are you of the same religion or different? If different, which religion will be the one in which you raise your children?
- Is he a drinker and partyer and you are not or vice versa?
- Is his background similar to yours?

Women are motivated by a number of factors, ideals, goals and external pressures. For example, until very recently, Mother Nature limited our years to have a family and this forced a number of bad relationship decisions.

The Story of Luna

Luna is a smart, educated woman who met the man she would marry in her mid twenties. She is a tenured professor and he is in pharmaceutical sales. It seemed like a good match, but while she became very well respected in her profession, he did the bare minimum to get by with his base salary. She wanted to be the best in her field while he was happy to keep the status quo even though he was with a great company that would have rewarded his efforts handsomely. At the beginning, she found his detachment intriguing. He was creative and different from any other man she had ever dated, and this was very appealing. But now, after the house in the suburbs and the two kids, the appeal has worn away; in fact, it was replaced by frustration and waning respect.

When she thinks back to the beginning, the signs were all there. His friends were not successful, he didn't even own a suit, and he never spoke about his professional goals and ambitions. Early on in their marriage, she began to earn more than he did, and she didn't mind until he started doing less and less. One day she realized that she had been supporting the family while he went around dreaming up companies that never got off the ground. Ultimately this created an emotional chasm between them.

The problem was not that she earned more money than he did but that his lack of drive left her disillusioned. This, coupled with the stress of financially maintaining the lifestyle they achieved when both were contributing, while being a full-time mother to two children became too much for her. While she worked hard to make a name for herself, he became dependent on her and she realized that she was enabling him. A deep resentment began to grow. After 8 years of marriage, they divorced.

After much reflection, it became apparent to her that he didn't really want the same things out of life that she wanted. He felt forced to constantly raise the bar of his performance to the standard of living she, at that point, had become used to, and his heart was never in it.

He would have preferred to live simply, have few things, and work less. For her, work was a source of fulfillment and pride so she did not mind working hard to achieve her goals. Not only did he have to work harder than he had ever worked, he had to constantly and spiritually do the work of convincing himself that he *wanted* to work harder than he had ever worked before. That made the lifting twice as hard for him, while for her it felt like she was dragging a 200-pound weight uphill.

There's no reason for this unhappy outcome for two perfectly good people. Everyone should go boldly in the direction of the life they dream of, and no one should have to constantly compromise their ideals. There is definitely a lot of value in Luna's husband's way of thinking, but unfortunately it is not compatible with her way of thinking. The age difference also may have been an issue. Luna wanted to spend her 30's and 40's striving so that in her later years, after the kids went to college, they would be comfortably set. By the time they met, her husband had wasted most of his 30's and when the financial crisis of 2008 hit, it devastated him. He never fully recovered. Neither of them is right or wrong, neither is better or worse; they are simply incompatible – and if she had been honest with herself about what she wanted out of life *and* honest with herself about who *he* was, she probably would not have chosen him as a partner. She also had not thoroughly assessed what the life of her dreams was going to cost, emotionally, psychologically, or financially and what it would cost her relationship.

These are two people who felt whole but were incompatible. It is important to note that no one "completes" anyone. In other words, two half-persons do not make a whole. We have to be entirely who we are, always evolving, and in synergy with the evolution of our chosen partner. I see it as two concentric circles overlapping.

This is why the work of Chapter 1 is so important. From there, all of your decisions will spring forth. I don't have all the answers and this is not a foolproof plan, but the point of this book is to provoke critical thinking so as to facilitate the making of informed decisions, and possibly avoid years of pain and suffering.

Listen to What He Has to Say – And What Others Say About Him

Once you have sat with yourself and thought things through, talk to your partner directly about his values and visions of his future – and actually listen to what he says. You must also – and this is extremely hard – listen to what others are saying *about* your partner. The people closest to you have the distance to see what you can't see. Try not to get defensive. Take in the commentary and do with it what you choose, and then discuss with your partner some of the following notions:

- Do your profiles match, really?
- Are your most important needs and desires going to be satisfied, naturally, by who and what he is right now?
- Are you happy at the thought of tying your life to him, just as he is, or do you think you will change/improve him?
- Do you consider him to be your equal intellectually and socially?
- Is his vision of his future compatible with yours?
- Will he enhance your life or do you think he will "complete you?"
- Is there fundamental agreement between your two profiles about money, style of living, commitment to home and family, and parenting styles and expectations?

Research:

1. Jade Yap writes on *Tiny Buddha* about looking at your overarching views of what life is and what it should be – and how to shed preconceptions that might have been formed before you knew what you know today. http://tinybuddha.com/blog/getting-to-know-yourself-what-you-like-and-what-you-want-in-life/
2. A quick and useful quiz to assess whether you're living in and being unduly influenced by the past, or you're living in the present: http://tinybuddha.com/recreatequiz
3. "Want To Know Yourself Better? Ask Yourself These Questions," by Gretchen Rubin. https://www.psychologytoday.com/blog/the-

happiness-project/201206/want-know-yourself-better-ask-
yourself-these-questions

4. Andrew Moore does a great job walking you through an honest
assessment of your "couples value." He encourages an
examination of aspects of your dynamic as a couple that women
often tell themselves shouldn't matter, but do: Does he make a
good impression at parties? Does he get along with your own
family members? Given his current habits, do you expect he'll
still be attractive to you 20 years from now? "Assessing Your
Relationship's Value: How Much Is Your Relationship Really
Worth?"
http://www.askmen.com/dating/curtsmith_200/241b_dating_advi
ce.html

5. Randi Gunther, Ph.D., says there are seven dimensions of an
intimate relationship, and evaluating those seven areas is a good
starting point in evaluating your partner. "Seven Ways to
Evaluate your Intimate Relationship: An easy guide to see where
your partnership is thriving or just surviving," published in
Psychology Today.
https://www.psychologytoday.com/blog/rediscovering-
love/201304/seven-ways-evaluate-your-intimate-relationship

6. Katie Heaney and Chiara Hatik offer a somewhat tongue-in-
cheek, but nevertheless surprisingly useful quiz about your
boyfriend's value. The twist is you're supposed to have your best
friend fill it out. "Top Secret Forms: The Ministry for Boyfriend
Review," in *The Hairpin.* http://thehairpin.com/2012/04/the-
ministry-for-boyfriend-review/

Chapter 3

The Happy Couple

Now that you've looked at your values, wants, and needs, and his as well, it's important to look at how you two are likely to fare as a couple. Be Aware that the internal systems that you set up in your home from the onset will forge themselves into becoming your customs. I realize, again, that this is unromantic and that you probably don't want to think about all of this when you first get married, but you're building your foundation. It has to be solid.

Matches & Mismatches

First, examine the obvious problem spots – areas where you appear to be a mismatch; i.e. messy versus orderly; like to cook at home versus can't cook (or don't want to cook). The point is to figure out who is good at what and how you will divide your tasks. Some of this will happen organically, and that is totally fine too, but don't count on everything just falling into place. If you do, you may very well end up living a home life that is not only not the right fit for you, but that's seriously unhappy.

Consider each of these areas on your own first. How much are you willing to bend? What items are nonnegotiable?

Now discuss these areas with your partner. Talk about them honestly. Keep reminding yourself; it's either an uncomfortable discussion now or a full-blown battle later. Once you have children, you will really wish you had had the honest talk and listened to your gut about your compatibility.

Do also look at the areas that *are* a match. Talk about these too with your partner. Get specific. Be sure you are talking about the same things and that you truly understand what the other person is saying.

Finances

Next, be sure to have a very frank and practical discussion about financial matters. I hope that you did this before you became serious about making your relationship permanent, but even if you did, this topic is one that will ebb and flow and will need constant reassessment as your needs change. Even if you've talked about financial issues in the past, do it again now. Make a checklist of the following questions, and discuss them with each other in detail.

1. What's your expectation of income level?
2. What is your expectation regarding the type of neighborhood where you will reside and the schools your children will attend?
3. Do you feel that both partners should work throughout your income-earning years in order to bring in as much money as possible, or is home and time with children or each other or leisure more important than money?
4. Do you think you should combine your earnings and expenses, or keep your earnings separate and divide expenses?
5. What do each of you think about saving and spending?
6. What percentage of income do you think should go toward savings, vacations, home, clothing, charities, education, and helping family members?
7. How do you see your current income fitting into your expected expenses? Sit down and make an actual, detailed budget.

The reality is that almost no one does this in-depth work regarding money prior to marriage. I cannot think of a single person who has met with me to discuss the possible dissolution of their marriage, in my twelve years of practice, who reported conducting a thorough inventory of their relationship – especially their attitudes and expectations about money – prior to tying the knot.

Also, be very aware: once you are married, unless you have a prenuptial agreement, everything you acquire from the date of your marriage becomes part of your marital estate regardless of whose name is on it. This applies to assets – and – it also applies to debts. For example, if at the date of filing a petition for dissolution of marriage (divorce), you have a $25,000 debt at a department store that was accumulated after the date of your marriage, $12,250 is your partner's responsibility and $12,250 is yours alone.

This is why I cannot stress enough to you that you have to know what is going on with the money at all times. You need to know your partner's spending habits, you need to know how much he earns, and you need to know where he banks and what deductions he's taking out of his paycheck. And in fairness, he should know yours too. Finally, be very clear on this point: If you stop working by joint decision, *you are no less entitled to this information* than if you were working and contributing financially to the marriage. In fact, if you stop working, it becomes even more crucial to know what is going on with your family's finances.

I cannot tell you how many times I meet with women who do not even know where their husband of 25 years puts his money. This is most common among stay-at-home women. Believe me, I understand the desire to want to disconnect, and I often think that it would be nice to be able to let responsibility go and rely on someone else to take care of the financial aspects of a grown-up's life, but I can assure you that ignorance is *not* bliss. It never is, regardless of whether your husband is hiding money or doing you wrong or is totally honest and above board. It simply is, regardless of circumstance, downright frightening to be 50+ years old, or really any age, and not know if you have $1,000 or $10 million and whether you're responsible for debt of an unknown amount.

Sadly, the women who come to me with no idea where the money is and whether there's debt and, if so, how much, all say the same thing: "I feel so stupid." I've had clients, clueless about their personal financial circumstances, who once were VPs of Marketing or Directors of Development for large corporations. Some even had law degrees – but when they got married they were lured into the golden cage syndrome – believing that within a marriage, money was the husband's domain.

Hear this message: It doesn't matter whether your partner is fantastically successful or barely covering the rent. The reality is, you're still a responsible adult, and you need to act like one. The even bleaker reality is that when you're married, you can actually be made responsible for half of the financial effects of what your spouse does or does not do – think bankruptcies, plummeting credit scores, etc. And if you end up divorced, half of his dishonesty, or his stupidity, or his failure to earn or save can come to rest on your shoulders alone. If you left the marketplace, you may be in an even worse position because you may or may not ever be able to earn what you would be earning had you never stopped working. Never lose touch with this reality. I'll say it frankly: Don't equate being a married woman with being a stupid girl about money.

This is true in all cases, whether you work and earn an income or not. Don't be lulled into a state of powerlessness if your partner agrees with your decision not to work outside the home or has insisted on it. Being dependent on your spouse for your family's income does not mean you have to abdicate your power. You are one-half of that relationship, and unless you've signed a prenuptial agreement, the money that comes into your household during your marriage is your money as much as it is his. You have a right – scratch that – a responsibility to yourself, to know where it is and where it is going!

Children

Next comes the discussion of children. If you hope to have a happy family life and a stable home for your children, you must talk very openly about children before you get married, with as much detail and "what-if scenarios" as possible. Again, make a checklist of questions, and discuss them one by one openly and honestly. Be sure to cover at least the following issues.

1. Do you both want children? If so, when do you want to start? How many do you want to have?
2. What would you do if an unplanned pregnancy happened?
3. Would you rather focus on careers and income and maximize your ability to give the best education, lessons, clothing, camps, and vacations to your children, or would you rather focus on day-to-day time with the kids?
4. How does each of you see the other as a parent? Do both spouses agree on who should be responsible for things like missing a day of work to take the kids to the doctor – or sidelining a career path to stay home with kids?
5. Do you each see yourself as a parent whose kids admire your status

or enjoy the benefits of a high income, or a parent who values staying at home with the kids day in and day out, even if that means fewer luxuries in life?

6. What's your view on discipline and punishments?
7. Do you believe in public education or can you barely stand the thought of your children not enjoying the experience of a private school education?

One very productive way to insure that you cover all of these issues and discuss them in detail would be to attend a parenting class together – and use each session as a basis for a frank discussion. It is impossible to foresee every permutation but as before, the goal is to communicate and minimize outstanding issues before you have children.

Communication

Besides financial disagreements and arguments over child raising, a difference in style of communication, or even worse, a lack of communication, often leads to the demise of couples. In a healthy home, you should never feel afraid to voice your opinion. You should never have to worry that telling your partner your thoughts on a particular subject will cause him to leave you or become unduly angry. Disagreements, possibly even heated arguments, are par for the course of any relationship, of course, but these should amount to no more than a raising of the voice, never to threats of leaving or the raising of a hand.

The subject of domestic violence is a sensitive one and not covered in this book except to say that domestic violence – emotional, psychological or physical – is never acceptable and is always a valid reason to terminate a relationship. You should not be afraid to call the police, file a police report and press charges, when necessary. There is a cycle to domestic violence and it is possible to break the cycle. For more information visit womenslaw.org

Research:

1. "How to Talk About Money Before Saying 'I Do'," *CNN Money.*
   http://money.cnn.com/2013/06/13/news/money-marriage/
2. Dr. Amy Wenzel offers great tips to keep in mind as you think about

your financial compatibility, and lists four specific topics that definitely should be addressed, in "How To Discuss Finances With Your Partner Without Freaking Out," published in *Huff Post Weddings.* http://www.huffingtonpost.com/2013/11/04/marriage-finances-_n_4179498.html

3. Melissa Diem discusses 20 things you should definitely discuss before you get married, and the issue of children is number one on her list. "20 Things to Discuss With Him Before Marriage," in *All Womens Talk.* http://love.allwomenstalk.com/things-to-discuss-with-him-before-marriage

4. Dr. Laura Berman, Ph.D., discusses ten conversations you should have before getting married, in *Everyday Health.* Somehow the slideshow presentation of the 10 topics makes it all seem so clear. http://www.everydayhealth.com/sexual-health-pictures/dr-laura-berman-10-conversations-before-marriage.aspx

Chapter 4

Let's Make A Deal

Here's where the lawyerly outlook really comes into play to protect you. This is the point in your decision-making about your relationship that will create a stark dividing line between those who have the best chance of lifelong success and those who don't. It's all about "sealing the deal."

We already know that many, if not most, young couples devote little time to examining their relationship in hard, cold, practical, factual light. It's common for most people in love to assume that love will conquer all, that their passion-infused relationship will carry forward unchanged, and that no matter what obstacles come across their path, they and their partner will face them together as a team.

If you're reading this book, you've demonstrating that you're already one step ahead. If you've really put thought and effort and time into all the points and issues raised in Chapters 1 to 3, you're on the right path. And if you've successfully raised and navigated honest discussions with yourself and with your partner, and you've given even more serious thought to your partnership in light of those discussions afterward, bravo. You've come a long way forward from what I'll politely call here "ignorant bliss."

But you're not done.

This is where you put your money where your mouth is, where you put on your "big girl panties," where you take your hopes, dreams, and promises and bring them firmly and squarely into the land of reality. Seriously. And this is especially true if you will always work and if you have great earning potential and perhaps your future spouse does not. More and more we are seeing women out earning their mates, and as a result in the 21st century, women are paying alimony, not just receiving it.

It's time for you to consult with outside experts, those who aren't in love with you or your spouse and who are well versed in legal, financial, and relationship matters.

The first step is to tell your partner that this is what you want to do, and be prepared for push-back, even if every discussion up to now has been open, calm, rational, and pleasant. Your partner may take offense at the whole idea that you feel you need legal or relationship counseling to enforce the decisions you've made together and the promises he's made to you. After all, don't you love him? Don't you believe he loves you? How can you be in love and yet have no faith in his goodness nor trust that he'll really keep his word to you?

Don't fall into this trap. And that's easier said than done. After all, this can feel for so many to be a great, cataclysmic, crashing collision between love and selfishness, faith and distrust. Your partner's expression of hurt feelings or anger may not only be sincere, but quite innocent. It's entirely possible that there's not a hidden agenda whatsoever or any private feeling that he doesn't want to be obligated to you or he doesn't intend to honor all of the decisions and promises that he's made. Despite his good intentions, it's just a sad fact that he may feel, in his gut, that relationship counseling or a legal contract have no place in a love relationship. This is especially likely if he comes from a family background in which outside counseling is never used, or written legal documents are rare, such as a family in which loans among friends or family members are vaguely defined and never reduced to writing, or decisions to go into business together are sealed with nothing more than a discussion over dinner and drinks. The whole concept of getting outside advice or putting anything into writing may feel foreign and cold and even aggressive to a person with such a background.

But the real, pure logic is this: What's the harm in confirming what you've clearly discussed and decided on? Think of two of the oldest and clearest pieces of wisdom gleaned from hundreds of years of human business dealings: The best way to ruin a friendship is to go into business together, and the best way to protect a business relationship is to write out a detailed legal contract that provides for not only all the plans and promises for the business but the particulars of its demise, should it come to that. Now, I grant you that a marriage is not a business deal, but it is a merger and involves your well-being, your fortunes, your day-to-day life, and every path you will take in life. It's more serious and more far-reaching than any mere business deal ever could be.

I'm not saying that you should sit down and hammer out a pre-planned divorce agreement to have at the ready for an inevitable demise of your union. Rather, I'm saying that it's smart – so smart – to put your best, most fair, most rational decisions – the ones you've worked so hard to agree on up to this point – into writing – now, when you're at your best and most hopeful and when you haven't been thrown into a state of stress or anger or disappointment by the vagaries of life. Why not care for one another, and for yourselves, by putting your best conceived plans and decisions into writing, with provisions included for what you will and will not do in the event that plans go awry? Why not? What is there to lose? Of course, there's everything to lose when you're throwing your lot in with someone else. Why not go all in, 100%, to make it as good, free of misunderstandings, and successful as it can possibly be? Where is malice or hurt or harm in that?

Counseling As The First Step

Whether your partner is balking at the idea of bringing a third party into the picture or not, consider the benefits of premarital counseling before you go any further. Honestly, have you come to perfect harmony on every single issue you've discussed? Be totally honest here, not only about the resolutions reached or not reached, but the level of mutual agreement on those issues where the two of you have "agreed" on something that started out from different points of view. Is it possible you agreed to something you really didn't feel good about? Or might he have agreed to something that maybe really doesn't sit well with him, but that he said yes to because he wants to please you? A good counselor can guide you through not only areas where you know you don't agree, but those areas where maybe you're kidding yourselves, a little or a lot, about the mutual understanding you thought you'd come to. Discussions with a counselor can be very enlightening, and since they're conducted in a safe environment and with the wisdom of your counselor's training and years of experience, you can be helped considerably, sometimes in ways you didn't even know you needed. Sometimes, too, simply the environment and mood created by a counseling situation can bring out a greater willingness to be fair and consider the other person's view.

You'd be surprised at how often a wise counselor can provide some proposed solutions to a problem or clash of views that you hadn't thought of yourselves. And a lasting benefit is that a counselor can give you some operating guidelines for navigating areas where there just is never going to be perfect agreement. You can use those tools time and time again over the years.

Perhaps the best outcome from premarital counseling is the valuable training you can get in how to fight fair. This overarching value – being respectful, honest, open, and thoughtful when there's a disagreement, no matter what the disagreement is about – can be the saving grace of a marriage that isn't perfect, but is worth saving.

So how do you find this wonderful, beneficial, and wise counselor? Here are seven steps you can use to guide you:

First, take care to choose a counselor who will satisfy the requirements of one or both of your religions, if this is important to you. Talk to a pastor or rabbi or other religious leader from your faith(s) to find out what is required.

Second, check with your insurer and find out if counseling is covered by your policy, and to get a list of counselors covered by your program.

Third, look for a specialist in pre-marital counseling – not just marriage or family counseling. You can of course do research online; you can also contact the American Association for Marriage and Family Therapy (AAMFT) and ask for a referral to a credentialed specialist.

Fourth, check out your potential counselor's background; degree, years in practice, whether any complaints or disciplinary actions have ever occurred. Check out websites where patient testimonials are posted. As with sites like Yelp, such testimonials must always be taken with a grain of salt, but the number of testimonials and the occurrence of repeated, similar complaints - or compliments - can be helpful. Ask trusted friends and colleagues for recommendations.

Fifth, it may sound obvious, but sometimes it's lost among the other considerations: Choose a counselor whose location and office hours are convenient for both you and your partner. Bad timing, traffic, disruption of work and so on can make convenient, and tempting, excuses to quit counseling, especially if sessions might be feeling uncomfortable to one party more than to the other. Don't set yourself up for such obstacles.

Sixth, make sure you start your relationship with the counselor by discussing, up front, the treatment plan. How often will you meet for sessions, how long with the sessions last, and what will you expect during your meetings? Some counselors prefer to start with an assessment process and lay out goals that you'll work toward. Others want to hear your backgrounds while others start right off the bat with a more open discussion, and ferret out weaknesses and issues as you proceed. Make sure you're both on board with the style and direction of counseling you're going to receive.

Finally, be upfront about the fees and expect the counselor to be the same – not only how much she or he will charge, but how much will be covered by insurance and how that coverage will be collected. Many counselors will not deal with their clients' insurance companies directly; they expect you to pay them at the end of each session, and they will give you a form to submit to your insurance company for reimbursement of the insurance company's portion of the fee. Be clear on how the process will work, what will be coming out of your pocket and when, and be sure you're comfortable with the arrangement and able to meet the expenses.

Pre-Nuptial Agreements:
For Good Relationships, Not Bad Ones

The way to think about pre-nuptial agreements is that they're the embodiment of "do unto others as you would have others do unto you." In the best of worlds, you would have your partner do everything he could to insure that he will, not only now but in the future, respect you, treat you fairly, and honor the promises and commitments he makes to you today. In the best of worlds, he would seal that future not just with a kiss but also with a specific, detailed, and binding agreement. If you love him and sincerely intend the best in life for him, you would do the same for him too, would you not? Why not love yourself enough to expect this from him and love *him* enough to provide the same protection *for* him? A pre-nuptial agreement is an act of love, care, and faith, not suspicion and selfishness.

You, your partner, and everyone else who's going to have a voice in your dealings have to get over the bad rap that pre-nuptial agreements have been given. For most people, the term conjures up the classic scenario of the wealthy old man and the young bimbo trying to take him for all he's worth.

OK, such scenarios do exist. Pre-nuptial agreements are protective of that classic old man who's got a lot, and therefore a lot to lose, and who stands a high chance of being taken advantage of by a conniving young woman who's targeted him for his money. Often in those situations, the parties know the deal that they are making and those unions are typically temporary.

But let's try another analogy. Presumably you wear a seat belt every time you're in a car. Does that mean you believe that you're going to get hit by another car, or ram into the back of a truck, or drive off a cliff during your drive? No. You actually, fervently, and continuously believe that you won't suffer or cause any harm whatsoever. But you wear that seat belt anyway. Why? You do it because you can't tell the future. No one can. Unfortunately, bad things do happen sometimes - and somewhere in the world, the country, your town, someone gets hurt in a car every day. Because, god forbid, yes, it could happen to you. And despite the fact that with all your being you do not want anything bad to happen to you, you do acknowledge that it could, and you do care for yourself enough to protect yourself, ahead of time, as best you can. You buckle that seat belt.

Bear in mind too that pre-nuptial agreements are not just about divorce; they come into play in the event of the death of a partner too. Sometimes you or your spouse may want to insure that the other receives property or protections, in the event of death, that might not normally fall to them as a spouse; or conversely, there may be family heirlooms or other rights or property that you want to insure stay with the family of origin even if they would normally pass to your spouse in the event of death. A pre-nuptial agreement will settle such matters calmly and rationally ahead of time.

Your pre-nuptial agreement is your buckled seat belt – for you, for your partner, for the children you may eventually have. It helps protect everyone against unnecessary pain and suffering. It's a good thing.

It's not necessarily a protection against the wife taking from the husband, either. More and more, women are out-earning their partners. Can you see yourself paying your husband alimony? Think about the history of such divorce awards; they're founded, historically, on the old and now outdated model of the husband breadwinner and the mother housewife/child caretaker, a model created in a time when women, for all practical purposes, were unable to earn a decent income and were unavoidably financially dependent, 100%, upon their husbands. In this classic situation, if the marriage ended after years of the wife caring for the family home and the children, it was only right that the husband should continue to support her financially at least until the time that the children became adults and could fend for themselves. After all, her work and actual caretaking significantly affected his ability to earn a good living and have a family and enjoy a good home life.

Now that model doesn't exist across the board in such black and white relief. Yet often, awards of alimony are made to the non-earning or lesser earning partner at the dissolution of a marriage whether or not the lack of earnings was the result of the partner bearing other responsibilities or providing other benefits to the breadwinner over the years that precluded earning an income. It is often unfair. Husbands who simply didn't care to work much (or at all) and who did not, in fairness, then take care of the lion's share of household and child raising duties have been, and still are more often than you might think, awarded alimony simply because, it seems, they didn't earn much of anything while they were married; therefore they are not very employable and need support when they divorce. In practical effect, they've been rewarded because they've been lazy and they've let their wives do pretty much all the work.

Whether such a situation could or would arise in your life, the fact remains that in most cases, the earnings of the husband and the wife will not be equal, and the division of household responsibilities and child-raising duties will not be handled in equal proportion either. Things may be inequitable, and maybe that's OK during your marriage – however you've worked things out is, I hope, how it feels best for both of you. But if your marriage comes to an end and you're faced with dividing up all of the assets, assigning future ongoing financial responsibilities, and making decisions about your children's future, equality and fairness should be insured. And the best way to make sure things will be decided fairly is to decide them when everything and everyone are at their best – meaning now.

Inequities in earnings and responsibilities could happen in your marriage – even to the point of serious imbalance. You just do not know, for certain, what will happen as the years go by. Of course, you don't believe there will be inequities, but there could be. So just as you click that seatbelt every time you get in the car, for god's sake, click this seatbelt too before you take the biggest ride of your life. Get a pre-nuptial agreement in place before an "accident" can possibly take place.

But hey, aren't prenups still just for celebrities and rich folks? Why should "normal" people with "normal" incomes get them? Robert DiGiacomo writes in Bankrate.com about why every couple should get a prenup; not just celebrities and rich folks. "Any couple who brings personal or business assets to the marriage can benefit from a prenup. The most basic of these contracts lists an inventory of premarital assets that in the event of a divorce will remain the property of their original owner," he says. For example, does one of you own a timeshare, club membership and/or investments? Will these be brought into the marriage and considered both of yours, or will they be kept for only the spouse who purchased them? Prenups don't have to be lengthy or complicated. They just have to be clear.

The other important element is spousal support. Here is another area where your work in Chapters 1 through 3 will come in handy. You need to be able to talk things out openly and honestly with your future partner. Again, it's those same discussions about whether you will work or not. The alimony schedule and other agreements that you devise in the prenuptial agreement will affect your life in the future if there's a divorce or death, so you need to be able to try to project to a time that you probably have no experience with yet. It's also a good idea to talk to other women and ask them to share their experiences with you. There is no replacement for experience, so reach out!

So what's in a pre-nuptial agreement? What's the purpose of it? Is it all about expectation of failure, or does it deal with more positive issues and can it feel good, not bad, to negotiate all the terms and make your decisions together? See the checklist at the end of this chapter for the essential elements of a pre-nuptial agreement.

A few last thoughts on the subject: Give yourself time. I cannot stress this enough. Ideally, you should give yourself 6 months. You should be very conscious of your sense of self and self-protective instincts when you're working out the details of the agreement. Avoid the pitfall of "over-willingness" – being anxious to sign anything and everything that your partner asks, to "prove" that you're all about love, not money. And don't let yourself be shamed or intimidated into leaving out provisions that you know are important, out of a fear of seeming too concerned with money or rights to property down the line. It's all about fairness, and there's no fairness if one party's interests are favored over the other. So, know your worth, keep a level head, be practical and truthful, and employ the services of a trusted family law professional to keep the process productive and even-handed.

And how do you find a good lawyer, one who's written many pre-nuptial agreements and will make sure that yours covers all the bases, complies with all laws, and will stand up to the test of time? You might have a good recommendation from a friend or family member. But if not, one excellent resource is the "Find A Lawyer" section on the American Bar Association website. Whomever you find, be sure to check that lawyer's background and look him/her up on websites that rate law firms and lawyers and provide client testimonials.

Finally, know that while I've given you all of this detailed advice and reasoning for pre-nuptial agreements, I don't discount for a minute the difficulty of bringing the whole subject up with your partner in the first place. You might need to get help with just that, to start with. Pre-marital counseling would be a good place to broach the subject. Or, a trusted and wise friend or family member might be the person to consult about not just the need for a pre-nuptial agreement but the best way to bring the subject up with your partner. Think about the initiation of the process very carefully, and lay the groundwork with thought and care before you start.

A CHECKLIST OF ESSENTIAL
ELEMENTS OF A PRENUPTIAL AGREEMENT

1. A prenuptial agreement must be in writing.

2. Aim to have your agreement signed at least 60 days prior to your marriage.

3. Each intended spouse should have his or her own lawyer. Never agree to dual representation.

4. Exchange a copy of each other's credit report.

5. Conduct a full disclosure of your financial circumstances and demand to receive full disclosure with sworn affidavits, bank statements – all types (checking, savings, money market, certificates of deposit), pension and retirement account statements, stock (vested and non vested), bonds, personal tax returns, corporate tax returns, copies of any trusts that your partner is a beneficiary of, etc.

6. Decide which assets will remain separate property, as if the marriage were not taking place.

7. Decide which debts will remain separate, as if the marriage were not taking place. (A debt should always follow the asset.)

8. Decide which existing asset will be commingled with your marital assets, if any.

9. Carve out a special mention for the marital home; for example: If one uses premarital assets to make the down payment but pays the remaining mortgage with marital funds, will the property remain

non marital or will only the amount of the deposit amount be "owed" back to the person who paid it at the time of a sale or distribution?; or will the marital home be marital property subject to equitable distribution, regardless of how it was obtained?

10. Decide how you will handle income. Will employment income be marital or non-marital? Will employment income from certain sources be non marital and from certain sources be marital? Will income from non marital assets be considered non marital or will the income be marital, just not the corpus of the asset?

11. Address the way you will handle tax liabilities. Will you file jointly or separately? Is there outstanding tax debt?

12. Think about credit issues, such as credit card use, pledging your home as collateral, using home equity lines of credit to fund businesses or repairs or to get by in a tough economy.

13. Will all debt accrued during the intact marriage be considered joint or only if both parties signed off on the debt?

14. What are your expectations about the jobs and income you will each have? What are your views on working, raising children and managing the household?

    a. Are either or both of you on a career path that may require moves? Whose career will take priority?

    b. What if one of you changed careers and made substantially less than your earning potential?

    c. Does one of you have a risky career where the chances of a disability are greater?

    d. At what age do you plan to retire?

15. Spousal support is a tricky area and where a lot of disagreements manifest. Whether or not one party will work or stay home to raise the children is a major consideration. Also, think about whether there will be a large discrepancy between the parties' income even if both are employed full time. You don't have to

address it in your agreement, but most people do. In any event, you should definitely talk about it. Consider the following:

a. Will you both work or will someone stay home with the kids?

b. Do you want to agree to something different than what your state laws provide for?

c. Do you want to limit the amount, duration and terms of the support to be paid?

d. Will you use percentages to determine the amount or a fixed number – lump sums or monthly amounts?

16. Gifts from family and wedding gifts are another hot button issue because at the time of a separation, the family member who gave the gift will not want it to benefit the other spouse, and the tensions rise quickly, so spell it out in your prenuptial agreement and avoid the stress later.

17. Self-employment and independent business ownership are also areas with special issues to think about because many small business owners have a lot of discretion over how much of the corporation's gross income is taken as salary or income for the corporate offices and employees.

a. Should the business owner indemnify the other spouse from any liability relating to the business debts, taxes, personnel, back taxes, payroll taxes, etc.?

b. How does the business owner determine income in a subchapter S corp at the time of the agreement?

c. Should you make provisions for a forensic accountant to conduct an evaluation in the event of a divorce or separation?

d. What happens if the business owner opens a subsidiary? Will the subsidiary be considered part of the marital estate even if the parent company is named as a separate asset?

18. You should meet with an estate planning lawyer soon after you are married to insure that you carry out the intent in the prenuptial agreement, and definitely after you've had children, but in the event of a divorce, what will happen to your estate?

   a. Do you care if your spouse inherits from you if you're separated but haven't filed for divorce?

   b. What happens if you die while you are happily married?

   c. Do either of you have children from a previous relationship to consider in your estate plan?

   d. Do you have life insurance – is it whole life or term and will your spouse be the beneficiary?

   e. Will your surviving spouse be able to maintain his or her lifestyle in the event of your death while you're happily married? Will either of you have immediate access to funds if one of you dies? Will either of you be able to maintain your home if the other dies?

   f. Will the surviving spouse waive the right to take an elective share?

This is not an exhaustive list and different circumstances will require different provisions. This is intended to be a starting point and a guide for negotiations.

Research:

1. *Wikihow* gives a simple 7-step basic guide to finding a good premarital counselor, at http://www.wikihow.com/Choose-a-Premarital-Counselor

2. Margarita Tartakovsky, M.S., discusses the benefits of premarital counseling, and – perhaps most useful – lists the top reasons why couples skip it. Finally, she offers several practical pointers in how to choose a good counselor. http://psychcentral.com/blog/archives/2015/02/20/the-benefits-of-premarital-counseling-how-to-find-a-therapist/

3. *Hitched* also offers six tips for finding a marriage counselor who's right for you, in "How to Find a Marriage Counselor" by

Francine Kizner. http://www.hitchedmag.com/article.php?id=243

4. The famous (or infamous, depending upon your outlook) Dr. Phil shares the essential elements of fighting fair, in "How to Fight Fair." http://www.drphil.com/articles/article/20

5. Merriam-Webster defines a pre-nuptial agreement as, "an agreement made between a man and a woman before marrying in which they give up future rights to each other's property in the event of divorce or death —called also *pre*nup*, \ pr - n p *prenuptial*." Although the man/woman reference is a bit outdated, the definition is useful, in that it references the use of such an agreement in the event of death of a spouse – not just if there's a divorce. http://www.merriam-webster.com/dictionary/prenuptial%20agreement

6. In a *Business Insider* article entitled "Here's Why Every Couple Should Get A Prenup Before Marriage," Libby Kane discusses one of the main benefits of a prenuptial agreement: open, honest communication and decision-making now, when you're most in love with each other and haven't yet run into snags in your relationship. http://www.businessinsider.com/every-couple-needs-a-prenup-2014-8

7. Robert DiGiacomo writes in Bankrate.com about why every couple should get a prenup; not just celebrities and rich folks. http://www.bankrate.com/finance/personal-finance/engaged-couples-sign-prenup-1.aspx

8. You can get an idea what a prenuptial agreement might look like at *Rocket Lawyer*, where you also can download forms and create your own agreement if you so choose. However, drafting such an important document on your own without a lawyer's input is not what we advise. This document deserves the training and expertise of a lawyer versed in the laws of the state in which you are getting married. https://www.rocketlawyer.com/form/prenuptial-agreement.rl

9. Other than the recommendations of friends and families, there are several excellent resources for finding and learning about the track records of lawyers who can prepare a prenuptial agreement for you. Here are a few: the "Find A Lawyer" section on the American Bar Association website, http://apps.americanbar.org/legalservices/findlegalhelp/main.cfm?id=FL; http://www.lawyers.com; and http://family.findlaw.com/marriage/prenuptial-agreements.html

PART TWO

You've Tied The Knot: Now What? Marriage

Chapter 5

Establishing Self-Sufficiency

You're married now. You've navigated successfully through all of the soul searching, questions, discussions, revelations, and honest assessments, and you've gone forward with marriage. Congratulations on being so in love. If you've also hired and given time and attention to third party professionals as we discussed in Chapter 4 – counselors, religious advisors, accountants, and attorneys – and you've allowed them to advise you regarding your finances and your relationship, congratulations too on working so hard to make your marriage a healthy and happy one. You're on your way.

Now it's time to get down to brass tacks and make here-and-now decisions. The first one is whether you will continue to earn an income now that you're married.

This isn't a yes or no question. Your answer may or may not be the same depending upon time and circumstance. So I advise you to consider this question carefully right now, and revisit it whenever you're facing a major life change such as the decision to have a baby, or a possible relocation for a new job or promotion for you or your spouse.

Of course, whatever the circumstance, there is no "right" answer that applies to all women uniformly. Perhaps you're a professional who's worked hard (and spent money) on earning your credentials and developing a career in your field. Or perhaps you've never pursued a higher education. Maybe you're someone who's always gone after financial and career success with gusto, or maybe you're a person for whom work and earning money have never been the driving force in your life but rather a necessary responsibility that you must bear in order to take care of all of life's needs. The type of person you are will most definitely affect what's right for you. Don't lose sight of your own personality and outlook on life; make decisions that are right for who you are, not who others think you should be.

So think about who you are now; or rather who you were when you came into this marriage, before you decide what to do going forward. Know your own desires before making assumptions about what you will or should do now that you're a married woman. For example, do you feel that both you and your husband should earn money no matter what, full steam ahead, building on financial strength and security from Day 1? Or do you feel that the partnership of a marriage is an opportunity to allow one person to pursue his or her dreams (an advanced degree, the launch of a new business, an artistic or acting career) while the other pays the bills and supports the partner's goals? What do you see for your own greater good? What do you see for the good of the family that you've now become?

Think through the following scenarios and examine your "happiness and hope" factor, i.e. the feeling you get in your gut when you imagine living them through:

- At work you maintain your forward momentum with the same energy as before. You stay as involved as you've been in the past with co-workers, activities, and chances for advancement. You not only accept invitations to go out to lunch with co-workers, you often do the inviting yourself, even though it means spending money. You accept invitations to meet after work for a drink and sometimes you yourself suggest drinks or a quick bite to eat even though it means time away from your husband. You throw your hat in the ring for chances to attend conferences or take on new projects to advance your career.
- Or you pull back a bit, continuing to work right now just as you have been doing, with no change in plans or direction. Your main goal is to stay employed right where you are. You don't pull back on relationships with your co-workers, but you do invest less time and effort than you did before in maintaining them or developing new ones. You go out to lunch or out for a drink after work if asked but you don't extend invitations yourself. If chances come up to attend conferences or take on new projects, you'll most likely accept the opportunities if they're offered to you, but you don't actively seek them out.

- Or, you pull back significantly on your level of activity in the outside world, concentrating instead on leaving work when the day is done and coming home to build your home life with your new husband. You avoid spending money on socializing with co-workers and you turn down opportunities for new projects that may mean more hours at the office or chances to attend conferences that mean traveling out of town.
- Or, you lay low, privately planning your exit strategy, knowing that you plan to have children and quit your job once you have your first baby.
- Or, you aggressively seek advancement at work, going after recognition, promotions, and every opportunity that could enhance your career and your income. You take on a supercharged attitude toward your work, now that you're done with the dating game and the uncertainties of life as a single woman.

Don't get hung up on what you think you should do, which is admittedly hard to do in this day and age. The world is your oyster and there are no restrictions (at least hypothetically there aren't any) on what you can or can't do, which is wonderful and, to be honest, stress-inducing at the same time. Your upbringing, your rosy plans for the future that you had in earlier times before the realities of life came into play; the articles you read about women and careers; the television shows you watch portraying women in powerful roles; the discussions and advice that are heaped upon you by the media; all point in every direction that you could imagine for your future. In other words, they point nowhere. So, bottom line, you have to decide for yourself. What's right, actually, for you?

Don't forget, when you're considering all of your options, the power dynamics inherent in the question of who earns money and how much. If one of you will be the sole breadwinner or one of you will earn substantially more than the other, will you both be able to honestly subscribe to the notion that you're equal partners in the marriage with an equal voice over where you live, what kinds of cars you drive, what quality of clothing you'll wear, how much you put into savings and how lavishly you entertain and take vacations? And if your spouse has all or most of the earning capacity, will you be able to make clear and free decisions about everything from how often you go to the hairdresser to whether you will stay or go if the relationship fails? Money is power. Don't ever forget that.

Research Your Options

It's time to conduct major research into your options. One by one, research and record your answers to the following questions:

1. If/when you do have children, how much maternity leave can you take? Do you know how long you'll forego an income for pregnancy and maternity leave? Do you know how women are treated when they do take maternity leave? Is their career thrown off track? Are they given lower level work when they return to the office or passed over for promotions down the line, or are they treated the same as before they had children?
2. What are your husband's options for taking leave if you have children? Does his workplace have a paternity leave policy? If so, do men typically take advantage of it without consequence or is it frowned upon, even though the company officially provides for it?
3. Do you plan to share childcare equally, even to the extent of both of you working permanently reduced hours? What will that do to your income?
4. If you or your husband work reduced hours, how will you and he feel about that decision? Good? Self-directed? Or resentful, denied your dream of rising like a rocket in your career?
5. Do you plan to stay put, or is one of you likely to want or need to move for career/family reasons? What will that do to the career/earning capacity of the other?
6. Is more schooling in the future for either of you?
7. Do you or your husband want to pursue creative interests, and are you both willing to give up an income to make it possible?
8. Are either of you self-employed? Do either of you want to start a business?
9. If you don't earn an income, can your husband afford to maintain you at the level that you wish to live – i.e. will you be a Target mom or a Neiman's mom?

All of these questions boil down to two questions: how much money will you have and how much control will you have over your money? The answers to these questions, particularly the latter one, are answers that separate the women from the girls. Are you going to be in charge of how your life turns out or are you going to abdicate all power to another or to fate, whatever that is?

Most likely, all of your life you've subscribed to the view that "money doesn't matter when you're in love." That seems the morally correct view, doesn't it? Sure, but there's a big difference between consciously choosing one man over another (or over staying single), knowing and therefore choosing that you will have less money, and blindly making decisions without regard to the financial consequences. Being blind to money is not choosing love over money. That's choosing to be irresponsible.

Know this: Finances are one of the leading causes of marital troubles. Doesn't that tell you that finances are the most important part of *staying* in love – more important, even, than fidelity, at least statistically speaking? So be a grownup and do all of your research, and then talk with your spouse about all of the possibilities, focusing on the financial aspects of each.

Your math skills are as important as your verbal skills here. Go one by one through the questions above with paper, pencil, and calculator or an excel spreadsheet at hand. Here's how:

Work Out A Real-Life Budget

For each question above that's a "yes" or a "maybe," work out what your income and expenses will be (as best you can), and rough out a budget operating under the choices you've made. If you've never done a budget before, here's a quick how-to:

Make a list of your monthly fixed expenses, and put the dollar amount next to each, like this:

Fixed Expenses
- Rent or mortgage
- Property taxes
- Utilities (phone, gas, electric, water, sewer, trash service)
- Food

- Insurance
- Car payment(s)
- Credit card debt payments
- Other loan payments
- Fuel, car upkeep, bus/subway fare
- Medical expenses
- Taxes (if self-employed)
- Emergency Savings

Now make a list of monthly discretionary expenses, and put what you feel is a reasonable dollar amount next to each:

Discretionary Expenses

- Entertainment (restaurants, theater, sporting events etc.)
- Hobbies & recreation
- Clothing
- Gifts
- Travel
- Investment Savings

Add up your fixed and discretionary expenses and write down the total.

Now add up your income:

Income

- Husband take-home pay
- Wife take-home pay
- Owner draw from a business
- Interest & dividends
- Freelance work
- Income from any other sources

Add up your total income and write down the total.

Now subtract total expenses from total income. If the result is a positive number, your budget appears to be healthy, assuming that all the numbers you've estimated are close to reality. If it's a negative number, then you need to either increase income or reduce expenses until the final sum comes up as either zero or a positive number. Otherwise, you will be going into debt each and every month and that debt will mount, and guess what – you'll be in financial trouble. That's a fact, not something that will take care of itself.

Here's where true adult behavior is a must. You must realize that the budget exercise is not a homework assignment that you can do incompletely or poorly; there is no grade of "C" where money is concerned. You can't add up your numbers, come up in the negative, and throw up your hands and say "I hate money. This doesn't work. Why even try. Forget it." Well, actually, to be perfectly accurate, you can, of course, and many do. Those are the folks who end up in financial trouble; they have mounting credit card debt or overdue bills and they're constantly stressed about money. You can join them if you like.

But if you want to be free of financial stress and worry, you have to accept that you're not done with your budget until you get an "A," a grand sum total of income minus expenses being greater than or equal to zero. If your numbers add up to a negative, you will be in the red. You will. You cannot accept this and figure it will "all work out somehow." It won't, I guarantee you.

You must – I cannot stress this enough – you *must* keep working with that pad and paper or that excel spreadsheet and adjust those numbers on the budget until you have a healthy and realistic budget. This means you will have to make real-life choices that will change the way you are going to live: choices about the size and location of your home, the amount that you and your spouse will earn, the kinds of cars you will drive (or if you'll take public transportation to save money), whether you'll join a health club or choose jogging to stay in shape, and even when or if you will have children. Money affects how you live. How you live affects your money. Make choices that both of you can happily live with and choices that will keep your financial picture healthy.

Who Wears The Pants In The Family?

After you've arrived at a "zero or above" budget, sit down and have a frank discussion about control of the money, whether or not both of you or just one of you are earning an income. Does staying home for the children, for example, mean relinquishing any power over the family money (It should not ever mean that.), or will you stay on equal footing? Even if you decide to not work, please do not abdicate your place at the table.

The Story of Nina

I can tell you the story of my client Nina. She and her husband were so in love when they got married. She came from a middle class family and his family was very wealthy. He bought her beautiful jewelry, designer bags, and other luxuries enjoyed by those with wealth. They had a son and at first everything seemed perfect. They travelled a lot so he convinced her that with his income and his requirements to be away from home frequently, she not only did not need to work, life would be easier and better if she didn't. So she quit her job.

When their son started school it became harder for her to always travel with her husband, but this change did not slow him down at all. While he was gone he would leave her spending money and she was authorized on one of his credit cards. Suddenly she realized that she had no idea where he banked. She had no idea how much money they had or how to access any of it in an emergency or simply because she wanted to. She had dropped out of college, hadn't worked in over seven years, and did not have access to all of the money that presumably came into their family.

Then their relationship started to deteriorate. She started to see his generosity for what it actually was – a way to control her and keep her under his thumb. She wanted out and she wanted out fast but it seemed nearly impossible because she had no control over her money. For years she had been completely dependent on his good graces.

The positive news is that they had a prenuptial agreement. Pursuant to their agreement, in the event of divorce, her husband had to maintain her at the level she had grown accustomed to for a period of no less than half the term of their marriage. He had to secure a home for her and their child and he had to pay her a sum certain toward spousal support. Thanks to their premarital agreement, she had enough time to get her life together – finish college, get a job, or work on starting her own business if and when they separated. This certainty and guarantee of her financial security gave her the power to make the decisions that were right for her.

Many women are not as lucky.

The point is that regardless of who earns the money, you should always have access to your family's income. It is your responsibility to keep yourself in the know about what is going on in your home.

Research:

1. Laurie Essig, a contributor to *Forbes*, makes a persuasive case, bolstered by statistics, for why women should continue to work after marriage, in "Does Marriage Demand Women Quit Their Jobs?"
http://www.forbes.com/sites/jpmorganchase/2015/07/23/from-storm-to-stem-rebuilding-xavier-university/

2. *U.S. News & World Report* offers a helpful article on how to prevent fights over money in their Personal Finance section.
http://money.usnews.com/money/personal-finance/articles/2012/09/06/the-best-ways-to-prevent-money-arguments-with-your-spouse

3. In a lengthy and beautifully written article in *Psychology Today*, Hara Estroff Marano writes about love and power, and says "Only equally shared power creates happy individuals and satisfying marriages."
https://www.psychologytoday.com/articles/201312/love-and-power

4. Imagining what life will be like "after" and then preparing for it are more than difficult; it's like looking at a peaceful, clear running track, then being blindfolded, having all kinds of obstacles, noise, and distractions added into the picture after the blindfold went on, and then being told to run around the track as fast as you can. It's very important, and very helpful, to try to really see what that "after" is going to look like. If you plan to have children, for example, hearing from those who've been through the changes caused by a new baby is the best research you can do. Here's an amusing but frank description: Kylie McConville and Elena Donovan Mauer share their advice in "8 Shocking Ways Marriage Changes After Baby" in *The Bump*,
http://www.thebump.com/a/shocking-ways-marriage-changes-after-baby

Chapter 6

What Will Change & What Won't

Same Car, Extra Driver

Think of this car analogy: You've been driving your car down the highway for quite some time. You know how to drive and you're experienced at reading maps. You've been deciding which way to go for as long as you've been behind the wheel. And when you've needed gas or repairs, or you've felt the need to pull over and rest, you've done those things according to your own preferences and judgment.

Now you're sharing that car with your new spouse – but you're not just sharing the ride. You're sharing the *drive*. You're installing a second steering wheel on the other side; a second gas pedal, brake, and clutch. You've got *your* map plotted out; he has *his*. You've got your tolerances for how long you can drive at a time and how low you can stand to let the gas gauge go; he's got different tolerance thresholds. You have your rules for maintaining the car; maybe you always replace the oil the minute the maintenance light goes on in the dash, for example, but maybe he always drives another thousand miles because hey, the oil change warning light is a guide, not an iron-clad edict, and waiting saves money, doesn't it?

How can you possibly continue to move forward smoothly, or fast, or at all, even?

It's all about decisions before you start the ignition.

Decisions to Make Before You Start Driving
Where to live

Maybe you've been living together for a while before getting married, and maybe you're not planning on making big changes in your living situation right away. That's fine, but the thing is, you can be lulled into a false sense of "it's all taken care of" by not thinking into the future. Whether you live together already or not, things *are* different now that you're married. You each have legal rights and responsibilities that didn't exist before – and, despite your thinking to the contrary, chances are that one or both of you may be perceiving your arrangement and your expectations differently than before. Being married is, in fact, different from just living together. So whether you plan to make some changes right away or later on in the future when you plan to move or change jobs, changes will be coming down the road eventually, so think through and talk about these considerations now:

Which home will you live in: his, yours, or something wholly new? Give your thoughts full leeway here as you consider the alternatives. Obviously practical considerations are a must, such as cost, difficulty of upkeep, and distance from work, but other considerations are valid if they're going to affect your future happiness. Is the home one that you will enjoy living in? Does its style and layout suit you? Is it situated just where you'd like to be – in the suburbs, say – or is it too far from the city or too close to noise and congestion? If either of you lived in the home with another prior to your relationship, will that past relationship haunt you as long as you live there? Think clearly and lay your feelings out honestly. Now's the time to discuss them, when something can be done based on those feelings.

Will you rent or buy? Why? If renting, is that what you prefer for the long-run, or are you planning to buy a home as soon as you can get the money together for a down payment? Would you rather rent a nicer place and live well now, and take your time saving money to purchase a home, or would you rather live as frugally as possible, the sooner to afford a home of your own? Talk these questions through.

How to live

Before either of you assume that the living room is where you only entertain guests – or that it's where you have all of your fun, like with a pool table in the middle of it – talk it out. Draw a rough layout of the rooms of your home and perform the simple act of labeling them. Then under each label, list the activities you envision will be done in each room. Some may say, for example, that the master bedroom is where you will snuggle under the covers and watch TV together at night; others might say that a bedroom is for sex and for sleeping, and a TV positioned opposite the footboard is a sign of a marriage headed for the rocks. Get your opinions and your druthers out on the table before you start moving furniture.

What about extra space, like an extra bedroom? I worked with one client who had been harboring resentment for ten years because when she got married and moved into the home that her husband was already living in, he refused to move out of "his" office in the extra bedroom, even though she had her own business and worked at home on a computer all day (and also handled all of the household bill paying and paperwork), while his job was outside the home. The situation was in place when they moved in together and he'd always made her feel like she was asking too big a sacrifice if she made him give up "his" space so she could have an office, so for more than a decade she had been working in the guest bedroom at a small desk or at the dining room table, going back and forth into "his office" to file papers and print documents.

There are other issues: Will either of you have family that will visit? Will your home have a separate room for your guests or are you ok with your space's use being limited? Will you want your kids to have a separate playroom? Will you want live-in help? It's admittedly hard to know the answers to these questions when you haven't been down this road before, but try to envision the scenarios. And again, ask around, ask your friends who have lived through some of the experiences that lie ahead for you.

Then there's the infamous "man cave" question. Personally I see this concept as a holdover from the old days when the woman was supposedly queen of her castle and the man was the warrior in the outside world. In that scenario, everything in the home was exactly as the wife wanted it, leaving no room for the preferences or predilections of the husband. His only hope for a bit of autonomy over his living space was to lay claim to a "man cave" in the basement or garage, where he would set up his very own space with a big television, sound system, games, and toys. Kind of like a great big boyhood bedroom, really.

Let's hope this bifurcated view of home life doesn't apply to your marriage, and that the decisions about the layout, look and use of the home as a whole have been made jointly. If so, why does it seem right to turn over a "fun and games" room to just one person in the partnership? But if you're okay with the concept, or if you'll enjoy the so-called man-cave every bit as much as he will, or if your preferences and his are so widely divergent that frankly it would be better to spend a significant amount of your time at home in separate parts of the house doing your separate activities, then a man cave may be the best thing ever for both of you. Just make sure it's what you both want before you automatically acquiesce to giving over a big space in the home to his exclusive use, just because "that's how things are done."

The style to which you'll become accustomed

You know how most men will recoil – and even ridicule their friend – if they walk into another couple's guest bathroom or kitchen or master bedroom and see pink and lace and floral everything – super girly girl? Or what about the feeling you get when you enter someone's home and Every. Single. Item. Is. Just. So. Maybe you get the creeps about the cold and overbearing ruler of this home that you're visiting.

Talk through which kinds of décor and organization in a home make you feel comfortable or uncomfortable; what is esthetically pleasing to you, what's too messy or too sterile, what color palettes you prefer. Work on how you can blend your styles. Do you want the look of your home to be cozy or spare, eclectic or planned and coordinated décor, party-friendly or family-centric? Do you want your home to be a showcase or are you more about comfort and ease of care?

Talk about furnishings: Will you use what's newest of the furnishings each of you owns, or stick to everything owned by one of you because it all matches? Are you going to slowly acquire new pieces one by one, or pitch everything in a room – or the whole house for that matter – and furnish it from scratch? Do you prefer French provincial or super sleek Euro styling?

Believe me, it's never too soon to iron out some sort of consensus on how your house will look, whether you're furnishing it anew now or your redecorating will take place some time in the future. Get a feeling for what "feeling" you're going for so that you're on the same page when you do start fixing the place up and making it more and more your own.

Keepsakes and storage are big issues to iron out ahead of time. You may be surprised to learn that your new husband is quite sentimental about what seem to you to be the silliest things – a collection of t-shirts, for example. Don't disrespect his feelings or presume that you have the OK to throw out his belongings just because you don't see the value in them. What to keep and how to keep it are questions often loaded with emotion, so talk these questions through.

Then there's plain old day-to-day clutter. Tolerance levels can vary widely on this issue alone. Some may feel that a big wide breakfast bar just looks cold and lonely if it's not covered with newspapers, keys, mail, pens, and cracker boxes. Others can't stand to look at it if the beautiful granite surface isn't clear and clean. Clutter or, conversely, the rigid enforcement of an assortment of "this goes here" rules can drive either one of you absolutely crazy. Express what makes you feel happy and comfortable in your home, what rules, or lack thereof, you can learn to live with it, make fair decisions, and then honor them. And avoid the pitfall of falling into old habits the minute the discussion has faded from recent memory. Turn your promises to each other into new conscious habits, and stick to them.

Day-To-Day Life

There are several factors that go into each of your expectations about how life is going to be, now that you're married:
1. How you've been living up until now.
2. How you saw your parents live, and whether you want (consciously or unconsciously) to emulate them or surpass them.
3. Your picture of the perfect marriage and home life.
4. Your sense of entitlement or "ownership" of the other.
5. Your feelings of obligation and duty to the other.

It might be best to spend an evening talking through the answers to the above questions before you even begin making decisions about how things will be between the two of you with regard to your daily rhythms of life together. You might uncover some hidden presumptions, sources of hurt or irritation, or deep desires that you didn't know were there. With this basis as a foundation, then go on to discuss the following questions.

Questions to discuss, not assume

What's your lifestyle been like up until now, before you became a married couple, and do you want that to continue or change?

1. Do you expect that both of you will come straight home after work each day?
2. Do you tend to work late, or does your spouse? How will that affect you?
3. What about boys' night out and/or girls' night out? Is that OK with both of you?
4. How often do you like to have people over?
5. How often do you like to go out?

Special Times

Before the questions of special events and trips come up, discuss them now, when you're not likely to create hurt feelings or add fuel to the fire by appearing to spring plans or ideas on one another. Will you still go on that college girlfriends weekend every year, or stop going, or try to turn it into a couples weekend, or do both? Where will you spend Thanksgiving, Christmas or Hanukkah, and New Year's Eve? Will your husband continue to go on that annual fishing trip he's been taking every year with his buddies? Will you continue to pursue the classes and hobbies you've been involved in up until now? Discuss and plan ahead of time.

The Big Picture

By the time men and women get to my office, they have forgotten all the good, hard work they put into their marriage in the early years to make it work for as long as it did.

The reality is that living two lives together under one roof requires compromise, and compromise is work. Marriage, inevitably, is hard work and requires a series of recommitments to make adjustments, to bend and renegotiate and find new ground for compromise in order to keep it healthy and happy. The point is that the more you communicate, the better it will be.

Don't ever forget that it's just as important to keep an open mind about your partner's ideas as it is to persuade him of yours. Statistical chance alone tells you that sometimes his ideas will be the better ones, even if they push you outside your comfort zone – or maybe, sometimes, *especially* if they push you beyond your comfort zone – in a good way, of course. You may learn something new or expand your horizons.

The bottom line is, it's best to talk about all of these things before you're in the midst of them. There'll be better understanding between you, and more willingness to compromise.

Research:

1. Here's a short and sweet overview of the issues to consider when setting up your new home together: "Tips For Newlyweds To Set Up Their First Home," by Namrata Arora.
   http://www.bollywoodshaadis.com/articles/tips-for-newlyweds-to-set-up-their-first-home-1760

2. "12 Tips for Happily Combining Households" by Laura Gaskill offers many useful tips on setting up your home together.
   http://www.houzz.com/ideabooks/3778710/list/12-tips-for-happily-combining-households

3. *Glamour Magazine* creates a really frank discussion (no surprise there; hey, it's *Glamour*) about what will change after marriage. Highly entertaining – and very useful too.
   http://www.glamour.com/sex-love-life/2012/12/what-really-changes-when-you-get-married

4. In "9 Things You Should Never Ask of Your Husband" by Natasha Burton, *Woman's Day* offers an interesting – and pretty outdated – perspective on what should and shouldn't change after marriage in order to maintain happiness. But if you apply her advice to both sides – husband and wife – it makes pretty darned good sense. http://www.womansday.com/relationships/dating-marriage/advice/a1602/marriage-expectations/

Chapter 7

Yours, His & Joint

Dollars and Common Sense

This may be the most important part of keeping your marriage healthy, and it's worth every ounce of effort that you put into it. I'm talking about money: planning, deciding, and managing it. Money is the leading cause of divorce. If you can maintain peace in your relationship when it comes to spending, saving, earning, and sharing money, you're 80% of the way toward a happy and successful marriage.

Money is not evil, but what people can do with it and how they can mismanage it can be a killer of harmony and happiness. More often than not, when I roll back the clock with a client, I find that she and her spouse simply did not put in the time, in the beginning, toward planning and sorting and deciding everything they needed to figure out with regard to their finances.

I've learned in this business to not be impressed by the appearances people display to the world, because so many times when you look behind the curtain what you find is mountains of debt, no savings and financial disharmony. Living for what other people think of you is no way to go about having a happy life. It is important to have these conversations because we are all tempted at times to covet our neighbor's lifestyle. You and your partner can ground each other in those moments of weakness. If you don't talk about it and you don't know what each other's financial picture is actually like, you can't help each other to build a stable, solid future for yourselves and your children.

I've found in my work that most couples who thought that they'd discussed money, had actually discussed their generalized feelings about money without really talking about any practical applications. In other words, they said things to one another like, "Our children's education will be more important than anything else," or "I want everything we do with our money to be as a family, not as you or me individually," or "I don't need to have a fancy home, but I do want our home to be kept nice."

Those statements actually are good starters for a real conversation about money. It's good to begin with your overall statements of values and how you picture your life going forward. But statements like these merely lay the foundation for a real conversation. What do they mean in the nitty gritty world of here and now?

You need to translate your values and your feelings into the real decisions you'll have to make and live by, day-to-day. Put in the time, I can't stress it enough. It's the best investment you'll ever make. Maintaining a healthy relationship around money, where the lines of communication are clear, credit records are clean, and rights and responsibilities are clearly defined, is worth its weight in gold.

Bank Accounts – Joint Or Separate?

Will you have a joint checking account or two separate accounts? Decide, and then follow through: Go to the bank together to sign any necessary paperwork.

I would like to insert a note here about how you go about executing your decisions, and the importance of your choice of action. What you do now, in your first steps of money management, will inevitably color how money management will be perceived by the two of you in the future.

Let's take the matter of setting up a joint bank account. Suppose the two of you decided to have a joint account, and you take it upon yourself to go to the bank and open the account. You fill out the paperwork, provide the ID, sign a signatory form. The bank manager tells you to have your husband come in and sign a signatory form as well. You tell your husband what branch you went to, the name and account number for your checking account, and maybe even which manager to ask for to speed the process.

Guess what? The joint bank account is now your responsibility, at least in your and your husband's perception. If there are problems with the first book of checks arriving in the mail, or if you need to change the name on the account if you set up a trust in the future, or if you're incurring fees for inadvertently using your overdraw protection – whatever comes up – it's quite likely that since you took the responsibility of setting up the account in the first place, the two of you will likely assume that you're the one to take care of any matters that come up with your account in the future – including, perhaps, monitoring the cash flow, seeing that you never go into the negative, and even paying all the bills and writing birthday checks and so on.

I strongly advise that when you take those first steps such as setting up your first accounts, even though they may be just symbolic, you take these actions together as a team. Go to the bank as a couple. Meet the manager you'll deal with, as a couple. Fill out your paperwork and sign your signatory forms together. When you take your initial steps together this way, you set yourselves up to believe that you are each equally responsible for the management of your money. It's a good way to start out.

I would also advise you against letting all the responsibility fall on his lap. At all times, you need to know what is going on. There's also the practicality that with responsibility comes an equal feeling of entitlement, and although it can seem burdensome at times, it is far better to carry the burden and feel entitled to equal information and control along with your partner, than to live in the dark.

Paying Bills – All As One Or Each Separately?

Will you pay all the bills from a joint account? Or will you each take responsibility for separate expenses – you pay the mortgage, he pays for food and utilities, for example, each of you writing checks from your individual checking accounts. Or will you have a joint account for household expenses such as mortgage, taxes, utilities, food, and insurance – and then separate accounts you will each use for clothing, car repairs, recreation, dining out, and so on?

Who Is Responsible For What?

Whether you decide to have a joint account or separate accounts, what do you feel is each person's level of responsibility? Do you feel, for example, that it's your partner's duty to cover all the household bills with his income, and that your income can go toward discretionary expenses such as clothing and trips out of town? Or do you feel that you're every bit as responsible as he is to earn enough to cover basic expenses? Are you OK with the situation if neither one of you alone is making enough to cover all the costs of keeping a roof over your heads and your family clothed and fed? Or do you feel that at least one of you should be earning enough to cover all nondiscretionary expenses?

Savings Plans

This area is ripe for contention. How much of your income do you want to put into savings? Ten percent? Fifteen percent? Where will you put it – will you keep a "do not touch" base amount in your checking account? Or will you open a simple savings account, or contribute to IRAs or to a 401K plan? Will you go to a financial advisor and have him/her advise you on where to invest the money you save, or will you self-direct your investments?

And, finally, do you consider your savings plan inviolate – to be used only in dire emergencies, or will you regard the money as a nest egg, to be dipped into now and then when you want to buy a new couch or take a vacation?

Really talk through these issues. When you decide on how much to put into savings, plug that number back into the budget you worked out in Chapter 5, review the rest of the budget to see if any other numbers might have changed since the time that you initially set it up, and crunch the numbers again. Does your commitment to saving 10% of your income, or 5% or 25% - whatever you've decided – really work? If not, review the whole budget to see if other expenses might be pared down or eliminated in order to make your savings plan practical, and, if not, how much you can realistically commit to saving every month.

Do You Need Permission To Spend Money?

Different people have different comfort thresholds when it comes to spending money on discretionary expenses. In some relationships, the wife feels the need to "ask" her spouse for the OK when she's going to buy new clothes. Perhaps they've agreed to sit down and agree before spending any discretionary money. In other marriages, the couple may agree that they're free to spend money on anything they'd like, up to a certain monthly dollar limit. In some relationships, the wife might think it's exciting and romantic if her husband comes home with a new car as a surprise, while in another marriage, the wife would be infuriated if her husband plunked down tens of thousands of dollars on a car without consulting her. In still others, both spouses might be comfortable with each of them buying clothing, going to the hairdresser, and enjoying the occasional lunch with friends without need for a discussion about what they're spending, but when it comes to buying things for the home – furniture, draperies, even table lamps – some of which might actually be less expensive than a visit to the salon – they've agreed to discuss and agree before purchases are made. Many times I have seen the situation where the one spouse is put on a strict budget by the higher earning spouse. This tends to create a lot of stress for the recipient spouse because once she's spent her allowance she is typical afraid to ask for more even when her partner makes plenty of money. The recipient is essentially treated like a child on an allowance - that's the deal that is made in certain relationships.

Know the deal you are making. Be honest with yourself about the trade you are making before it becomes fertile ground for resentment and anger. Either you are a leader, a subordinate, or a team member; it's important to know the role you are playing. In some relationships, these roles may shift around a bit but I would suggest that striving to be a team with your spouse, in the end, is the most rewarding of all.

Talk about dollar thresholds you feel should trigger a discussion before money is spent. Talk about types of purchases – regardless of the price – that you feel strongly should be made by mutual agreement. Be as specific as you can be.

And finally, for all of those iffy areas that you didn't cover in your talks, I advise you to both agree to err on the side of over-sharing and excess caution when you're thinking about spending discretionary funds. It's much better for the health of your relationship, and for your ongoing trust of one another, if you talk first and spend second, rather than if you spend money that you assume your partner won't object to, and then you end up fighting about it.

Mad Money

Beyond all of the types of purchases I've been discussing, are the little things that really don't amount to much of anything on their own, but of course can add up. A coffee at Starbuck's, money for the parking meter, a book on Kindle, a smoothie… These all fall under the category of "mad money." What can your budget handle in the way of withdrawals from the bank to keep cash in your pockets so you have a little mad money when you need it? Figure out how much that would be, and pay attention when you go to the ATM to make sure that you stay within your limits.

Credit Reports and Scores

It's time to bring out your credit histories and put them on the table for full inspection. Let me advise this to start with: Come at this task from a position of love and understanding – both for each other and even for yourself. One of you will have a better credit score than the other. One of you might even have a score that's, frankly, in the crapper – and if so, chances are that the one with the bad score hasn't even looked at his or her credit history in a while because it's so painful to do so. If this is you, this is the time to tell yourself you have a partner now – someone who loves you and will stand beside you as you work together to make your score better. So stop wringing your hands, sit down, shut up, pay attention, and look at what's there. Whatever it is, it's there whether you look at it or not. Better to know what's on your record than to live in fear of what you think it might be.

It's easy these days to get your score and a full credit history. Many credit cards provide a credit score now on every monthly statement. For your full report, go online to a site such as annualcreditreport.com, creditreport.com , freecreditreport.com, or to the sites of any of the three credit reporting companies: Experian, TransUnion, or Equifax.

Be sure you understand how each of your credit histories will affect the other. Talk to your attorney, accountant, or even your banker about this. For example, if you're applying for a loan and one of you has a poor score, your chances for approval may be better if one of you applies individually rather than if the two of you apply jointly. Frankly, in my view this is nonsensical when the loan is for a fixed amount, such as a mortgage or a car loan, since each of you would be jointly and severally liable for the balance. How does it hurt the lending institution to have both rather than just one of you obligated, even if one of you has a poor record of paying off debts? But that's how it works; there's a "taint" that can attach to certain financial applications that you would be well advised to be aware of, if this might be an issue for you.

Debts

Do you have debts to pay off? Or perhaps, statistically speaking, it might make more sense to ask, what is the amount of the debts you have to pay off? Most people do carry debt these days, so don't beat yourself up about it. But do bring an adult attitude to the discussion. Debt perhaps is unavoidable, such as with a mortgage, but it is never just plain old good. Whatever the debt, wherever it came from, whatever the amount – it's good for your financial, emotional, and sometimes even your physical health to work toward paying it off.

Make a list of all your debts. Compute a total. Make a plan for paying those debts off, and try your best to be reasonable about what you really can do. If you're on a tight budget, for example, you stand a much better chance of successfully paying off that $800 debt if you schedule monthly $40 payments for 20 months, than if you decide to send in a payment today of the $150 you happen to have in your account and you "hope" that you'll be able to come up with the rest of the balance pretty soon. When you go that route, you wipe out your cushion today, which sets you up for a shortfall tomorrow that might require you to borrow more money and start the cycle all over again.

Credit Cards

Do you each have your own credit cards? Do you want to add each to the other's cards, or keep them separate as-is, or do you want to close your current accounts and open one or more joint accounts together? Credit cards probably are the most dangerous things to share between a husband and wife, especially if one of you has a problem with running up debt, so be very careful about your decisions. In the hands of someone who cannot control his desire for instant gratification, a credit card is the magical, perpetual "yes – don't worry – we'll deal with it tomorrow."

Even if your husband's credit record is good and his spending habits appear reasonable, be aware that if you add your husband's name to your account, he could run it up to the limit tomorrow, and you'd be liable for the balance. You might not think he would ever do such a thing, but if he's an authorized user, he does have the legal right to do so. He might not even intend to run up the balance, but through life-long habits or impulsive decision-making, he might edge it up day after day and bit by bit until it's maxed out before either of you realize it.

Finally, a note of caution even if you decide to keep separate credit cards. Debts incurred after marriage can result in liability for both of you, and this is true even if expenditures are made with one spouse's individual credit card in his name only. For this reason, it is essential that you each know what's going on with every credit card that's in either or both of your names. Make sure you know what cards your husband has, with what banks, what the account numbers are, and how to access those accounts online so you can review expenditures, payment histories, interest rates, and the balances. You should check this information carefully on your credit reports periodically as well.

Insurance

There can be wildly varying viewpoints on what is and is not needed in the way of insurance, so sit down and discuss this thoroughly with your spouse. And before you do, you might want to pull some numbers together first. Find out, for example, how much the premiums might be for different amounts and types of health, home, disability, life, and auto insurance before you sit down to figure out what's right for you.

Before you start adding up numbers, talk about what you feel you must insure. You might know that your own parents have set up a trust fund to pay for your children's college expenses, for example, so you know you don't need to provide for college expenses when choosing your life insurance benefit amount. Or you might have a large extended family with strong commitments to caring for one another in times of need, so you might feel that long term care insurance isn't necessary. Talk about these general what-if's first.

Then, one by one, review the following types of insurance, discussing what you're required (by law) to have, what you want to have even though it's not legally mandated, how much and what type of coverage you feel you need, and how much your policies are going to cost you. Then come up with a total cost and plug that back into your budget and see if your budget still works. If not, make adjustments until the budget balances again.

Types of insurance to discuss:

     a. Life insurance (term or whole life or both)

     b.Short term disability insurance

    c. Long term disability insurance

    d. Home & property insurance

    e. Mortgage insurance

    f. Liability insurance

    g. Auto insurance

    h. Medical insurance

    i. Extended care insurance

Hand-Outs

You might not like this term, but it is apropos for situations where others – family, friends, adult children – hold out their hands, literally or figuratively, and ask you to give them money. And note: This includes even situations where friends or loved ones ask you for a loan. More often than not, loans among friends and especially between family numbers eventually become gifts, because they never get paid off. Accept that risk and be prepared to shoulder it before you agree to give your money over to someone who's close to you.

So what will your policy be regarding hand-outs?

This is a very sticky area, because it tends to play on the heartstrings of some and set up a grim resolve to resist from others. How does each of you feel, in your gut, about a request from a friend for help when he's in financial difficulty? Is your reaction one of resentment: You manage your money, why shouldn't he? Or is it one of near-guilt: How can you say no, when you have the resources to help and this person you love is in trouble? If it's your adult children, will you feel that you can never refuse them, no matter what, since you love them unconditionally? Or do you feel that the best way you can be a parent is to make it clear that you expect them to stand on their own two feet?

Talk first about how you feel, acknowledge your feelings honestly, and then hammer out a policy that both of you can live with. A couple with opposing views might be able to agree on keeping a secret "trouble money" fund that they know is available if someone comes to them for help, for example. This allows the bleeding-heart spouse to be giving and caring, while also allowing the hard-hearted spouse to put a limit on just how far this giving and caring will go. Another possible compromise, if you don't want to set aside an account just for this purpose, could be to agree ahead of time that if someone comes

to you for help, you'll promise one another never to make promises to
another before discussing the matter together first.

Health Care

You may think of your health care decisions as individual decisions
that each of you should make on your own, at least with regard to
medical checkups and preventive care, but they really aren't separate
matters, because your health affect's your spouse's life and vice versa.
So before you get settled into a real routine, do sit down and talk about
what is important to you, not just for your own health care but for your
spouse as well.

Do you believe in getting annual check-ups, or do you think it's
better to avoid doctor visits if you're feeling fine, and go to the doctor
only when something is wrong? How does each of you feel about the
other's preferences in this matter?

Do you know your wishes – and your spouse's – should a medical
emergency occur?

What kind of medical insurance do you feel is right for you? Do you
want the highest coverage so you will know exactly what your
expenses will be per year, even though your premium will be high? Or
do you want to save on premiums and take a lower level of coverage,
so that if you don't in fact have a lot of medical expenses in a year that
you have to cover until you reach your deductible limit, you could save
money?

Do you have living wills, health care directives, medical care proxy
documents, and powers of attorney for one another? If not, do you feel
they're not necessary – or do you agree that you need them, and will
you make a plan to visit an attorney and get these documents in place?
If you do have these documents already, do you know where they are
and how to use them if needed? Bear in mind that a perfectly drafted
and properly executed legal document does you no good if you don't
understand it, don't know how to access it, or don't know how to assert
your rights pursuant to the document when needed.

Once you've had these discussions, make sure your documents are
organized together in one place, and that you both know where they
are and how to use them if you need them. Make extra copies so you
can grab a copy for the hospital if you need it and still retain the
original. Finally, make a family health calendar that designates dates

– or at least months – when you will schedule check-ups and tests that you've both committed to having each year.

Technology has made it so easy to do this. You can use a Google calendar and insert an event such as March 24th – Annual Check up for ACDC, and select "Repeat Annually" so that every year you are reminded to set an appointment. You can do this for each member of the family.

I keep a dry-erase calendar board in our kitchen by the back door, and every month I put in special dates, important meetings, birthdays, etc., for everyone to see every day as we go in and out of the house. My husband and I also keep the information in our phone calendars and then we invite each other to the events. For example, when I have my monthly board meeting in X organization, I insert it in my phone calendar and then invite him to the event. This way, he knows that he has to check our childrens' homework that night because I will be home late.

Research:

1. The *Wall Street Journal* ran an interesting pro-and-con article on the issue of separate versus combined finances in marriage: "Should Couples Keep Their Financial Assets Separate?" http://www.wsj.com/articles/SB100014240527023043607045794172514793 05712

2. Experian features a detailed list of articles on the ways that marriage will or won't affect your credit, and what you can do to make sure you can continue to have a strong credit report. http://www.experian.com/credit-advice/topic-credit-and-marriage.html

3. Whether or not you may be responsible for your spouse's debts depends upon the state in which you live. *NOLO: Law for All* explains more about this in "Debt and Marriage: When Do I Owe My Spouse's Debts?" http://www.nolo.com/legal-encyclopedia/debt-marriage-owe-spouse-debts-29572.html

4. For a good overview of what kind of insurance you should have at various stages of your life, see "Here's The Type Of Insurance You Should Buy At Every Age," by Libby Kane for *Business Insider*. http://www.businessinsider.com/insurance-for-every-age-2014-6

5. For an informative article that may help you if you struggle to get

your husband to go to the doctor regularly, read "Top 5: Reasons Why Men Don't Go To The Doctor," by Michelle Sobel in askmen.com. http://www.askmen.com/top_10/fitness/top-5-reasons-why-men-dont-go-to-the-doctor.html

6. Here's a recommended schedule of regular medical check-ups for men, according to *Men's Fitness*. The article by Carol Sorgen discusses what's needed and how often, broken down by age group. http://www.mensfitness.com/training/check-ups-every-guy-needs

7. For a general overview of recommended annual check-ups and screening tests for both men and women, see this overview article by the Center for Advancing Health: http://www.cfah.org/prepared-patient/get-preventive-health-care/do-you-need-a-yearly-checkup

Chapter 8

Follow the Money

Pay attention here. Your decisions about money management don't end when you decide whether to split expenses or share them or whether to keep separate accounts or set up joint ones. No matter what you decide and no matter who's name is on what, it is your right and your responsibility to keep tabs on what's going on.

Be aware that this is true for several reasons:

Worst case scenario – your partner is wasting money, hiding money, or lying to you about his money. If you have access to all of the accounts and you're monitoring them regularly, it's monumentally more difficult for him to get away with whatever he's trying to do.

Middle scenario – your partner is not paying attention to his money; how much he earns, how much he charges on the credit card, or how much he takes out of the bank using his ATM card. He doesn't seem to feel responsible to adhere to any kind of budget. I once had a client whose husband regularly forgot to deposit his paycheck, leaving their checking account without the funds that she had expected would be available when the bills were due. If you're monitoring the inflow and outgo and you can see whether the two of you are depositing paychecks and sticking to your budget or blowing it, you can call attention to problems and, it is hoped, work with your husband to rectify them before they really get out of hand.

Best scenario – your husband is honest and transparent in all of his financial dealings, he's depositing his income into the agreed accounts, and he's paying attention to how much he spends and on what. In this case, you're tracking and keeping tabs on all of your mutual financial transactions simply because it's smart to have an accurate picture of your financial position at all times. My mother always told me, "If you're not organized with your time and money, you'll never have enough" and she is right about that.

And, if you become the victim of fraud or stolen identity, your regular monitoring will allow you to catch unauthorized transactions quickly and be able to shut down accounts and alert the credit bureaus before the thieves have a chance to really cause a complicated mess for you.

There's one other scenario to consider, and that's when your husband is unreasonably fearful about money. He might have some deep-seated emotional issues surrounding money that weren't evident when you were dating or first setting up your home; perhaps he feels that no matter how much the two of you earn nor how well you adhere to your agreed budget, disaster is imminent. Or he may feel that anything other than the most basic of expenses are luxuries and therefore wasteful and immoral. If you don't know how much money you actually have and how well you and your husband are sticking to the limits of your budget, your husband's unreasonable attitude might lead you to believe that indeed you are in dire straits financially – and then you might allow yourself to be over-controlled and restricted when you don't need to be. Again, if you can check on the status of your accounts and see if you're maintaining expected balances, avoiding credit card debt, and building savings, you will be able to address your husband's over controlling or over-fearful nature from a solid position based on the facts of the situation.

Lastly, you should do it because it's the right thing to do. Grown ups care about and are involved in the day-to-day aspects of life. You should be too, even if you don't have to go out and earn the money you live on, because it will make you feel more accountable. A lot of marriages end when the provider feels taken advantage of or when he or she gets sick of giving and not being appreciated. Also, it keeps your mind active and involved in adult-level activities.

The Story of Catherine

I can recall being involved early on in my career in a mediation with a woman who had been a mid-level executive before she started having kids and chose not to work. She had full time help at home, so her life was basically one long play date, shuttling kids to and from, having lunch with friends, bearing no real responsibility for any aspect of her home. There's definitely something appealing to that scenario, especially, when your life is the exact opposite of that. However, it did not end well. Not surprisingly, after the youngest child went to college, her husband started divorce proceedings. And she was completely lost. Her husband was very successful and the kids were grown, so the settlement negotiations were purely financial in nature – the division of their assets and liabilities and alimony.

This poor woman had no idea where to start. She had competent counsel but I could see it in her face that none of it was making sense to her. It seemed as if a part of her brain had gone soft and she just could not piece it together – the analysis of her lifestyle, which lead to the analysis of her need, etc. It was sad to see that an educated woman had been reduced to the maturity level of a child. It wasn't that she wasn't smart; it was that she was completely out of touch with reality. And in her early 50's, she was starting over without the value of experience that she should have had by that point in her life. This is not an uncommon story.

Mad Money Versus Secrecy

In chapter 7, we talked about the advisability of each of you having a certain amount of discretionary funds each month to spend as you please. It's a good idea for both of you to have the ability to spend some money, no questions asked, without guilt. But there's a big difference between personal discretionary spending and secretive spending.

Let's say that you both agree to a limit of $1,000 per month for "mad money/no questions asked" spending, and let's also say that you've agreed to maintain separate checking accounts. The "no questions asked" policy means that if you take $1,000 out of your account, your husband has no standing to ask you how you spent it. If you happen to like indefensibly bad romance novels, a nice pair of shoes, manicures/pedicures and the occasional facial at your local spa, so be it. That's your fun and that's your right, up to $1,000 per month.

By the same token, if your husband wants to spend his money on Starbucks every day and sessions with a personal trainer, so be it. However, if he wants to go sky diving regardless of your strenuous objections, or take a female co-worker out to dinner and tell you nothing about it, that's not cool. Neither of you should feel compelled to report to the other on every dollar you spend, but you shouldn't equate the "no tell" rule with permission to spend money on activities or purchases that you know are violations of your trust in each other or the terms of your relationship.

So it goes without saying that checkbook registers, credit card bills, account statements, and online login credentials to financial accounts should be open and available to each of you, any time. If your husband doesn't want you to see the evidence of his financial transactions, think, why? There's no legitimate answer, ever. There never can be a good reason for hiding from your spouse what you're doing with your money. Who wants to live like that?

There is a sense of freedom that comes from being open and honest about your finances with your partner. No one is perfect, some are too tight and some are too quick to spend but if you approach it like a team sport then you can balance each other out and help each other.

Doing Versus Saying

You may agree with everything I've said in this chapter so far, but, like many of us, you also may be a person who likes to put off unpleasant or just plain boring tasks – tasks such as reviewing bank statements daily, weekly or even every month. If you let this predilection to put things off get the better of you, you might as well not have access to your financial records at all. Why? Because if you don't log into all of your accounts and look at them on a regular basis, and if your husband knows that you don't bother to do so, he might decide it's safe to go along hiding, taking, or wasting money right under your nose. And believe it or not, he might actually rationalize that it's OK to do so, because clearly you don't "care" about money. Or, he might simply be less disciplined than you are, and if you don't watch the store, so to speak, no one is doing so and that could mean you're heading for trouble.

Don't let either situation arise. Set aside a day or a night to log into your accounts, one by one. If it helps you face the task, set aside a nice bottle of wine to enjoy when you've finished the job. Just make sure you do it, religiously and regularly. With online banking being so prevalent and accessible, there really is no excuse for not getting to this task. Review the money coming in and the money going out. Are all of your husband's paychecks accounted for? Are the same bills being paid every month? Are there any unusual charges on your credit cards?

Are credit balances building up? Is money going into your savings or investment accounts as planned? Look, think, add up the numbers, and know what's going on.

You also should know what your obligations are – jointly and separately. Just because your spouse might be responsible for paying the electric bill, while you're responsible for paying the gas bill, doesn't mean that you shouldn't each know what both bills are, when they're due, what the amount of payment tends to be, and how to find the records if needed. What if one of you suddenly gets ill, has an accident, has to go out of town, or gets slammed at work? Be able to competently take over if and when needed. I recently represented a woman whose husband always paid the mortgage. For 16 years, he paid it monthly and on time but once the marriage was clearly over, he moved out and he stopped paying the mortgage. She was not in the habit of reviewing the household bills so she came to find out that he had stopped paying the mortgage only when she was served with a foreclosure notice.

Watch The Money Coming In Just As Carefully

Money coming into the household should be monitored as carefully as money going out. You should know what each of you makes in salary, bonuses and benefits. Not only is it good to keep tabs on the inflow, it's good to keep tabs on trends and timetables. What if your partner's employer promised a raise after 18 months on a new job, but the time comes and goes and no raise materializes? You might realize that your partner has failed to track the passage of time, so you remind him after the 18 months are up, to go to the boss to ask for that promised raise. Had you not said anything, that raise might not have materialized for months, or ever at all.

You also might uncover some aversion or fear issues, or a tendency to be manipulated by others, thanks to your regular monitoring. Let's say, for example, that the company your husband works for is having financial problems, and your husband has agreed to receive his paychecks up to two weeks late in order to help out with the boss' cash flow. Maybe your husband feels he's just being a team player, but you know that if he postpones income, you're going to overdraw your account or carry over credit card balances, which will cost you money in bank charges or interest. A sit-down might be in order to discuss the very real costs, to your family, of your husband's willing

accommodation to help out his boss' financial situation. You might
have some inkling at this point that money problems may be looming
on the horizon for the two of you, if you see that in a situation such as
this, your husband can lose sight of what should be his core values;
protecting hearth and home, when he's called upon to set aside his
own and his family's financial stability in order to protect someone
else's. Or you may find that after analyzing your cushion of savings and
the longevity of your husband's employment with this boss, it makes
good sense and might pay off in the future if you extend yourselves to
help keep the company going.

Thank goodness, in such a scenario, that you've been monitoring
cash inflow, because you've been able to spot the problem, the
potentially larger ramifications, and launch a discussion to make some
decisions and lay down some ground rules now, before more damage
is done.

There is also the occasion when someone gets involved with illegal
activity. If you know your family's spending patterns, you will know
immediately when suddenly there is an influx of funds that is fast and
furious or when dramatically increased spending is indicative of a
change in circumstances. I would think that you don't want to get
involved in those types of situations and that you don't want to have
your home rushed by the FBI one night while you're asleep in bed. I
know this sounds dramatic but I can think of several people whom I
personally know who've had this happen to them. If you have
children, this would be a traumatic experience to say the least, so you
need to know what is going on so you can extricate yourself from such
a situation.

Know Where Everything Is, And Where You Are

One of the most common issues I face as a divorce attorney is the
spouse - and it kills me to be gender-biased about these things, but it
is usually the wife - who comes to my office 100% clueless about where
her husband banks.

Please know what banking institutions are holding your money,
what types of accounts you have, what the account names and
numbers are, and how to log in online to check on those accounts.
Know too what you have in the way of money market funds,
certificates of deposit, safe deposit boxes, stock accounts, and

retirement accounts. Institutions, account names and numbers, phone numbers, and online login information – and in the case of a safe deposit box, the keys to the box – all should be accessible to you.

Keep your sights on the big picture, meaning your long-term plan. Evaluate whether you're sticking to it and achieving your goals. At the same time, remain open to reevaluating those very goals themselves if necessary. Things do change. Perhaps you're coming to realize that the schools in your area are not as good as you had thought, or maybe one of you has taken a jump in pay, making a bigger house than you had originally planned a possibility in the future. Or maybe now that you've had your first baby, your feelings about career and outside obligations have changed drastically and, to your own surprise, you've realized that you would rather forego a salary and the lifestyle it affords in order to stay home with your baby.

Maybe you're learning the hard way that home repairs, replacing appliances, keeping up with car maintenance, or saving for retirement are things you did not properly estimate or anticipate when you first sat down to plan your style of life and your budget. Don't despair or blame. Hey, everybody makes mistakes, especially those who are doing something new for the first time. Remember the race between Union Pacific and Central Pacific to build America's transcontinental railroad? They worked from the east and from the west, respectively, and were supposed to meet in the middle. But when the Central and Union crews ran into each other in northern Utah, instead of merging the lines right there, they continued building miles of parallel grading, with each company hoping to acquire more mileage and thus more payments from Congress. On they went, until Congress had to step in and set a junction point in Promontory, Utah.

Like that 1869 Congress, sometimes you have to admit that the path you laid out isn't the right one anymore, and you need to back up and move one or both ends of the track, point them in the right direction, and make them come together. The final route may not be exactly as it was envisioned at the beginning, but it's still getting trains from the Atlantic to the Pacific, so what does it matter that you had to make an adjustment in the middle? Life is fluid and you have to be able to ebb and flow with it; you have to be able to adjust.

You'll have noticed the overarching themes of this book by now: namely, *keep talking*, and *knowledge is power*. If you have thoughts floating around your head that you haven't expressed, or you're feeling tension or even just a change in mood that seems to be hanging over the two of you, bring it up. Talk about it. Good or bad, easy or hard, problems are better solved, one way or the other, than left festering.

Keep Checking On What's Going On

I talked in chapter 7 about checking your credit scores and credit histories, and I want to emphasize here that you need to look at these numbers and reports regularly; at least once per year, and with all three major credit reporting agencies. It's not good enough to check just one; you'll be surprised at what one agency lists that the others do not include, and at the varying scores that they assign to your record. Check them all, regularly, for both yourself and for your spouse.

Keep in mind this important fact too: Even though you may not be legally obligated for certain debts or obligations of your spouse, your jointly owned assets could be subject to seizure to satisfy them, so it's extremely important that you know what those debts are. And in the event of a dissolution, it's not just the assets that get divided equally, the debt does too. The more the debt, the smaller the net value of your estate, and therefore the smaller the settlement that you may be able to get.

Also know that the credit reporting agencies are notorious for mixing up credit records of people with the same last names, or who've resided at the same or even similar addresses. It's not just your spouse you're checking up on – it's the accuracy of the information the reporting agencies have on file. More than once I've seen credit card records of former spouses, former tenants of a residence, or even parents or siblings included on my clients' credit records, sometimes causing significant harm to their scores. Check those records and make sure that what's included in them is information only about you and that it's accurate and up to date.

Information on Credit Reports

You are entitled to a free credit report from each of the three credit reporting agencies (Equifax, Experian, and TransUnion) once every 12 months. You can request all three reports at once, or space them out throughout the year. Learn about other situations in which you can request free credit reports or to correct any errors you may find at usa.gov.credit-reports. Request your free credit report

Online: Visit AnnualCreditReport.com

By Phone: Call 1-877-322-8228. Deaf and hard of hearing consumers can access the TTY service by calling 711 and referring the Relay Operator to 1-800-821-7232.

By Mail: Complete the Annual Credit Report Request Form. It's available online at consumer.ftc.gov/articles/pdf-0093-annual-report-request-form.pdf as a PDF, which requires Adobe Reader to open. You can download Adobe Reader at get.adobe.com/reader/ and mail it to:

Annual Credit Report Request Service
PO Box 105281
Atlanta, GA 30348-5281

Research:

1. David Weliver provides a good set of guidelines on how to split expenses after you get married, in "How Do You Split Expenses With Your Partner Or Spouse?" published in *Money Under 30*. http://www.moneyunder30.com/how-do-you-split-expenses-with-your-partner-or-spouse

2. The Consumer Financial Protection Bureau lists instances when you should check your credit report, at http://www.consumerfinance.gov/askcfpb/312/when-should-i-review-my-credit-report.html

3. The Fair Credit Reporting Act (FCRA) requires each of the nationwide credit reporting companies — Equifax, Experian, and TransUnion — to provide you with a free copy of your credit report, at your request, once every 12 months. Visit annualcreditreport.com to get your reports.

4. CreditKarma.com provides free credit reports, free credit scores, and several online tools for managing your finances and your credit health. Go to https://www.creditkarma.com/

Chapter 9
The Relationship

I am not a relationship guru and relationship advice is not the point of this book. The contents of this chapter come from a compilation of stories I have heard and observations I have made over the years of couples that stay happily together and from the many lessons I have learned from the ones that did not make it.

Contentment Or Boredom?

What's the difference between reaching a comfortable equilibrium and boredom? That's a good question. Many define a healthy long-term relationship as being one of blissful boredom, or, in other words, compatibility with few sources of friction or disagreement. If there's nothing particularly wrong in your relationship but you're feeling as though it's stale or too predictable, *think about how you're thinking about it* before you decide that your relationship is in trouble. Can you change your negative thoughts about how predictable your routine is into warmer thoughts about the sense of security that you've come to trust over the time you've lived with your spouse? If you can change your characterization of your life together from boredom and monotony into a deeper, warmer attachment, you might be able to move your feelings toward an appreciation of the fact that your marriage has grown to a new and healthy stage. You have achieved "peaceful cohabitation." That's a very good thing.

Is It Him or Is It You?

On the other hand, maybe you really *are* bored – but with *your life*, not with your spouse. Your spouse may be just an innocent bystander in a life of your own that you've allowed to go stale. Are you doing work that you enjoy and that challenges you? Are you taking part in activities that are fun for you? Are you exercising and feeling good about yourself? Think about whether you've allowed your own momentum to slow down and whether you're blaming the feelings you have about your less than exciting life on your spouse.

The Story of Maria

One friend of mine complained for years that her husband didn't like to go to plays or the ballet – things she had enjoyed a great deal before getting married. In the beginning when they were together, he would show enthusiasm for such outings when she arranged them, and he seemed to have fun going with her. Then over time, he started "forgetting" about upcoming plans, and when she would remind him, he would act surprised and, frankly, a little unhappy that he was obligated to go – but when the time came, he'd gamely get dressed and get in the car. After a few more years, he started acting not only surprised when a date was coming up, but annoyed. He would ask her what the play was about, for example, and then roll his eyes when she explained. He wouldn't get dressed on time. He made them late more than once.

Finally my friend gave up, and stopped buying tickets to any cultural activities. They never went to the performances that she used to attend regularly. She felt sorry for herself that she had stopped being able to enjoy this important part of her life.

Then one day she met a new friend who, in the course of their conversations together, lamented that she never got to go to the ballet because her husband hated going. "So does mine!" said my friend. They came up with a plan to go together to the ballets that they so sorely missed.

"I wish that my husband liked going to the ballet and to see a play once in a while," said my friend, "and I felt very sorry for myself for a couple of years after I gave up on trying to get him to go with me." But once she met her "ballet buddy," she realized that her real sense of cultural deprivation and boredom came from not going to these performances, not from his not enjoying them. "Once I found a friend who loved the ballet as much as I did," she said, "I put ballet back into my life and I'm fine with going without my husband." Now she's looking for someone who likes to see an occasional play too. She's taken her life into her own hands and is actively planning to keep pursuing the things that make her feel inspired and rejuvenated, rather than letting her husband's lack of interest remove these activities from her life.

The point of the above story is that my friend had two choices: To decide that her marriage was dull and boring, and allow a feeling of discontent to fester, or decide that it was her cultural life that was dull and boring, and do something to change it with or without her spouse. Despite being a divorce attorney, I believe in the value of marriage and hope that this book will help many avoid having to go through the painful process.

The Scales of Justice Within A Marriage
Are you treating your spouse fairly?

The story of my friend and her desire to attend the theater and dance performances leads me to ask you a more general question: Is your attention to your spouse positive and supportive, or is it infused with resentment or disappointment? If the latter, is it really his fault? And do you have the power to change whatever is creating your negative feelings?

Many women have learned from their mothers – and from other female relatives and friends – that men are simply to be complained about. They don't pick up after themselves. They don't pay attention to them. They don't listen. They don't care. Such modeling can be very harmful. When a young girl observes the women in her life complaining in such fashion and doing nothing to change their lot in life, she can develop the idea that this is what a marriage is; a slow decline into a life with a man who becomes ever more neglectful and uncaring as time goes on. She believes that that's just the way marriage is.

You don't have to think that way – in fact you should kick yourself if you do. Back in the 40's and 50's, maybe such an outlook was unavoidable; after all, very few men would ever consider helping around the house or sharing in child care duties, and very few women were able to work outside the home in meaningful careers or professions. Options and expectations were very limited compared to today.

But you can and should expect a more equitable relationship, and if you're not happy with your husband, you should pinpoint exactly what is wrong, and set out to fix it. Rather than just accepting mistreatment or carelessness as if you're powerless, and going through life feeling resentful, you should speak up. Tell your husband what is bugging you, and what you would like him to do differently. He may be totally unaware of how he is aggravating or disappointing you, and might be more than willing to make some changes in order to make you happy. Give him that chance. The worst thing you can do, if there's a problem, is blame it all on him, seethe with resentment, and start treating him like someone you don't like. That's not going to change him into the person you wish him to be, and in fact it can only make things worse.

Always strive to voice any problems or concerns you may have, talk them out, come up with some mutually agreeable solutions, and give your husband a chance to treat you, or your home, in the way that you want him to. Your goal should always be to maintain a sense of peace and contentment in a home where you both are nice to one another. If that's not happening, don't accept it. Put real effort into making it happen.

Is your spouse treating you fairly?

Now let's turn the tables. Consider how your husband treats you and whether it's how you would like to be treated. Does he ask you how your day was as often as you ask him? Does he give you his full attention when you need or just want to talk, or does he keep the TV on or his laptop in front of him? Does he do his fair share of household jobs? Does he suggest doing things together that you both enjoy, or does he only make plans with his buddies? Is he nice to you, or irritable or uncommunicative?

If he's performing well on all fronts, kudos to you; you've got a good guy. But if you can see a pattern of declining interest, support, financial contribution, care, or fairness in pulling the load at home, speak up. You should never feel that it's "too late now" and you're stuck with whatever behavior he wishes to display toward you and your home. If you feel mistreated, ignored, unsupported, or unappreciated, do not simply accept that this is your lot in life. Speak up, state your feelings clearly, using concrete examples, and most important of all, tell your husband what you would like him to do or stop doing.

Communication
Make sure you're speaking the same language

I don't necessarily subscribe to the whole "Men Are From Mars, Women Are From Venus" mentality – that men don't ever give voice to their feelings and women just want men to give them flowers. There's lots more variety among individuals than that. But I do believe that there is a fundamental difference in the way that most women and most men express their feelings and solve their feeling-problems. Be aware of this and try to adjust your way of bringing up and carrying out a "feelings" discussion – not because you're trying to manipulate your husband, but because you're trying to get him to *understand* you.

In general, women tend to make statements, such as "I feel like you don't care about me anymore." And most men will be nonplussed when such a thing is said to them. A very unproductive and unsatisfying conversation can ensue from that opening salvo.

If, on the other hand, you choose an example of an action (or a failure to act) and you state how that instance made you feel, you will be bringing up a topic of conversation that your husband can clearly understand. You might be feeling unloved, for example, for a lot of reasons, one of which is that your husband never wants to go out to dinner with you on a weeknight – he never suggests it, and if you do, he always says no. Instead of expressing the general feeling that he doesn't love you or enjoy spending time with you, knowing that one example is this dinner thing, you might instead choose just the dinner issue to discuss. You might say, "When I was growing up, my father used to suggest going out to dinner, on the spur of the moment, at least a couple of times a month. We'd go out – not necessarily to a fancy or expensive place – sometimes just the hot dog stand a few blocks away. But it made me feel like he liked us – that he liked my *Mom* – that he liked doing something fun with us. I am feeling bad that you not only don't suggest that we go out for dinner once in a while, but that you say no every time I suggest it."

This conversation is based on a concrete example, and it gives your husband a chance to not only understand what you mean when you say "you make me feel bad," it also gives him a chance to do something concrete to change his behavior to make you happier. Finally, if it turns out that he's more inclined to hold up his hands and say "Whaddaya want me to do?" you have the opportunity to make a concrete suggestion that he might be able to live with – perhaps you can get him to agree to go out to dinner two weeknights a month.

The use of a concrete example provides another benefit, too. It may be that there's an underlying problem that gives rise to the behavior that you're complaining about, and this concrete example may provide your husband with a way to express the problem that *he's* having. Maybe your husband believes that the two of your are going over budget all the time, and the last thing you should do is waste extra money going out to restaurants. Or he might have a fear that you'll start demanding that you go out all the time if he says yes to you once or twice, and he doesn't want to have the daily uncertainty that he'll have to get up and go out all over again after he comes home from work expecting just to relax.

When you discuss your feelings around a concrete example, you have the opportunity to understand one another's underlying feelings and motives, and work out a solution. You might sit down with your budget, if money worries are the problem, and come up with a dollar amount that you both agree you can afford for weeknight outings. Or if your husband is worried that you're going to expect him to go beyond his "pain threshold" for going out on weeknights, you might agree that you will go out every other Wednesday, and all of the other nights he can rest assured that he can come home, change into his sweats, and stay put for the night.

Be nice

"Be nicer to me" was a sort of signal flare for my cousin and her husband whenever either of them felt they were being treated dismissively or thoughtlessly by the other. It was a little nudge. A "hey, who're you talking to here?" challenge, said in good humor. They seemed to always be aware of a "niceness meter" and they kept tabs on it. It served them well and kept them coming back to a place of warm and loving attention, or so it seemed to me.

Do you do any of the nice things you used to do for your husband when you were first together? Do you do anything new that adds pleasure to his day? I'm not necessarily talking about donning high heels and laying sushi on your naked body à la Samantha Jones in "Sex and the City." Maybe just buying some fresh flowers, as if life is happy and worth celebrating. Giving your husband an extra hug when you're cleaning up the kitchen together. Suggesting that the two of you go to a baseball game, even though baseball games are not exactly your favorite thing to do. Looking at him with a smile when he walks through the door.

It's amazing how these things can stop occurring to us when we're living a busy life full of responsibilities, especially when we live with a person who is just not as exciting as he used to be and who frankly, sometimes, irks us to no end.

But who wouldn't be less exciting with the passage of time, and who wouldn't annoy and offend on a semi regular basis when they live with you day after day? Does that mean that he doesn't deserve your love and appreciation for all the good stuff he brings into your life?

Think about how you treat your spouse day to day. Do you say thank you to him, when you would normally say it to others – or do you feel that it's not necessary to go to that trouble anymore, or maybe that it's just understood so why say it when he already knows?

Common courtesy is often the baby that gets thrown out with the bath water. Over time you become comfortable, routines become entrenched, he bugs you here and there and you annoy him from time to time. When you go through times of feeling that all is drudgery, or that you will scream if your husband clears his throat one more time, you may not feel like being particularly nice, so you aren't. And then when things get back to normal, maybe you just don't quite feel like picking up exactly where you left off. Maybe you stay silent when in the past you might have acknowledged a thoughtful act on the part of your husband.

Of course relationships do change over time, and you won't interact with one another after seven years together the way you did when you were newlyweds. But do stay conscious of the little courtesies and thoughtful gestures, and do acknowledge them one way or another. You may not want to say "please" and "thank you" all day long in a weird overly formal way, but maybe it would be nice to simply remark, once in a while, on something he does that you appreciate, like taking the trash cans out to the street every week so you don't even have to think about it. And some little daily courtesies might be good to keep alive. For example, if he still practices the habit of opening the door for you wherever you go – admittedly an archaic custom but charming nevertheless, can't you murmur a "thank you" each time? If you can't bother, why should he? Do be cognizant of the ways that he still works to treat you with love, respect, and fairness, and show him that you appreciate it.

Time Together

I know that every single book you will ever read about marriage will advise you to make sure that you spend time together regularly, just the two of you, before and after you have children. I believe that the reason it's always stressed so heavily is that it's rarely done. It's just not easy, it's sometimes hard to scrape together the energy, the money for a babysitter and an outing on a regular basis, and sometimes it's just not something you especially want to do. For harried mothers of young children, particularly, the desire to just be alone, alone, alone can trump every other wish you have.

That's OK.

That feeling does not necessarily mean that your relationship is dead in the water. Ask yourself why you're having a hard time carving out time for just the two of you, and see if you can remove the roadblocks. It may be a change in your feelings about the relationship, sure, but it's quite likely that it's some other problem having nothing to do with how you feel about your spouse. Remember that the two of you married so that you could be partners, lovers, friends, and a constant support for one another. You married because you had fun together. Don't assume that you don't have a good relationship anymore just because you aren't motivated to spend time alone. Maybe it's that your relationship is fine but it's the *rest* of your life that sucks.

If you're raising small children, for example, and you have no relief from your duties, try to find a creative way to get some time alone, just for yourself. Tell your husband that you'd like him to take the kids out with him every Saturday morning when he goes to the grocery store. Or if your parents live nearby, and they're available, tell them that you're having a hard time and ask them if they might come and watch your children one morning a week. If you have friends with small children, try to organize a schedule of swapping kids so each of you gets an afternoon off here and there. If there's a college nearby, maybe you can find a student who would like a child-sitting job a couple of afternoons a week on an ongoing basis. With your new-found "alone"

time, you'll probably be more interested in going out with your spouse
once in a while when you can swing an evening out.

Sometimes it's just money – the cost of hiring a babysitter and then
paying for dinner and a movie for the two of you every week is just too
much for your budget. In that case, even though you might prefer
evenings out as a way to spend time together as a couple, perhaps for
the time being you can enjoy some cost-free outings such as a walk in
a park on a Saturday afternoon. That brings your cost down to just the
babysitting expense. And if that's still a budget-breaker, maybe you
can trade off with another couple with small children and get away
for an afternoon at no cost at all.

Or the roadblocks may be in another area – a lack of shared
interests. After the years you've been together, you've each come to
realize – and admit – that you don't care for the activities that the
other finds fun: ball games, ballet, fishing, expensive restaurant
dinners. It's worth the effort to try to find something new that both of
you might enjoy; a culinary class, or renting kayaks for an afternoon,
a game of pool at a low-key bar, or a quiet afternoon at the local
bookstore having a latte and reading. Or you might find a modified
form of one of your preferred activities; instead of a ball game, maybe
it would be easier, cheaper, and fun for both of you to meet another
couple at the neighborhood sports bar where the guys can watch the
game and the women can socialize and enjoy the appetizers. That's
not exactly just the two of you spending time alone, but it is a "date"
without the kids.

It's possible that your lack of desire to spend time alone with your
spouse is due directly to his behavior toward you or the children.
Maybe your husband is a workaholic or unusually insecure at work,
and he always works late, coming home only when it's the kids'
bedtime. Maybe he's always too tired and hungry then, and he chooses
to sit in the kitchen stuffing his face while you give baths and read
stories to the children. Or maybe he tries to "make up" for failing to
come home in the evening by blasting into the children's routine and
playing with them and getting them riled up, making it twice as hard
for you to get them to bed, and making the children lose an hour of
sleep that they need before school the next day. If something like this
is the problem, you need to have a serious talk with your husband
about how his work habits (or other behaviors) are affecting your and

your children's lives. If he must work every waking hour of his day, for example, then perhaps he can find a way to bring his work home, and trade off that hour of stuffing his face alone in the kitchen at 9 at night with an hour eating dinner with the family and helping the kids with their homework before he goes back to his work while the children bathe and get to bed at their usual time. If your husband won't budge on altering his destructive behavior, insist on counseling or a meeting with your pastor or other advisor. When one partner is refusing to be a part of family life in a fair and constructive way, all kinds of serious problems can grow to gigantic proportions.

The whole goal is to not write each other off or consign one another to the role of the background set on the stage of your life. Keep trying to enjoy each other, even if the early days of unfettered time, early lust, and carefree fun are way behind you. Just because you can't have that relationship anymore doesn't mean you can't at least enjoy each other as friends for now. Remember that just as your early relationship has evolved into what it is now, it will continue to change as time goes on. The better you get along today, the better your chances are that upcoming changes will be good ones, and that your relationship will continue to strengthen, grow, and become more loving and even more romantic with time.

Summits

I talked earlier in this chapter about the importance of communicating, especially when feelings of discontent or resentment are rising up. There's another aspect of your communication that needs to be tended to as well; what I call summit meetings. These are conversations not about day-to-day affairs or problems that might be brewing, but about the Big Picture in your lives. Use your time alone, once in a while, to have conversations about where you're going, why, what your goals are, and how you feel about continuing on the path you've been on or perhaps changing direction.

How many children do you hope to have, and when? Have you started to feel that you don't want the larger family that you'd planned after all; that the two children you have is enough? Or did you think you were done having children but you've found lately that you really long to have just one more, despite your earlier plans?

Are you happy with the school that your children are attending? Are they happy, learning, and enjoying healthy friendships? Did you decide early on to provide the "best" for your children so you sent them to private school, only now you're starting to worry that the private school option is much harder on your budget than you had anticipated?

How about lessons, college savings plans, vacations? Is your plan for an early retirement likely to play out, given the amount that you've saved so far? Has a desire to start a new business made you want to dip into that retirement fund in order to pursue your new dream today? Or are you starting to feel that you aren't saving enough – or that the austere retirement savings plan you agreed to a few years ago is just too extreme and is making your current life bleak and dreary?

Talk about these big decisions regularly. Even if you discussed everything thoroughly early on and you came to some very clear agreements, always remember that nothing is ever cast in stone. Life just isn't like that. Allow for some regular course adjustments as you travel down the road of your life together.

When Storms Are Brewing

If you're having continuing problems or an ongoing mood of ill will, do speak up and do find a way to sit down and talk through what's wrong. This can be hard to do if you feel that your husband just doesn't care anymore or that he's hopelessly inconsiderate, unfair, or just plain lazy or selfish. After all, the very qualities that led to his bad behavior may make it very unlikely that he will listen to what you have to say, or care about what you say, or be willing to do anything to change.

But that doesn't mean that you shouldn't try. Remember, you can never change another person, but you *can* change your own actions, and at the bottom of it all, that's what such a discussion is all about. If there's a problem, you must change your current action – which is either 1) doing nothing as you resign yourself to your fate of living in a bad marriage, 2) acting out in equally negative ways to try to push your husband into becoming someone different, 3) saying or doing things to try to make his life as miserable as yours as you try to even the score, tit for tat, or 4) making your feelings known and understood, and then deciding what to do based on your spouse's actions, or lack thereof, after you've shared your feelings.

Be self respecting. Sit down with this person, your husband, whoever he is or has turned out to be, and tell him what he's doing or not doing that you have a problem with, tell him how you feel about it, and ask him to work with you to come up with a solution to fix the situation. Either he'll hear you, and commit to some concrete changes, or he'll share some problem of his own that's underlying his behavior, or he'll be impervious or hostile and totally unwilling to hear you or do anything about the problem. You actually cannot control or even predict which way this will go. But you can make clear what your feelings are, and why, and give him a chance to rectify the problem. And you can learn whether your husband cares or intends to change anything to restore the health of your relationship. And, armed with that knowledge, you can decide for yourself what you will do, yourself, going forward, to insure your own happiness and that of your children.

Research:

Here is a small selection of articles on how to evaluate the health of your marriage, and things you can do to keep it happy and strong:

1. "11 Ways To Make Your Long-Term Marriage Happier, Starting Today," by Shelley Emling and Ann Brenoff.
   http://www.huffingtonpost.com/2014/03/11/marriage-advice_n_4823414.html

2. This one's a doozy and should keep anyone busy for a while: "50 Proven Tips for Making Your Marriage Last."
   http://www.happywivesclub.com/50-proven-tips-for-making-your-marriage-last/

3. Jeanie Lerche Davis offers tips for being nice to your spouse in "Want a Happy Marriage? Be Nice, Don't Nitpick. True Compatibility Doesn't Exist, so Shrug off Little Conflicts."
   http://www.webmd.com/sex-relationships/features/happy-marriage-no-nitpicking

4. Matt Gannon discusses, honestly, the men's perspective on being a good spouse and keeping the marriage alive, especially after kids, in his article on *The Good Men Project*, "How to Hold Onto Romance After You Become Parents."
   http://goodmenproject.com/featured-content/how-to-hold-onto-romance-after-you-become-parents/

Chapter 10

Misconceptions of Marriage

It's Not All About You

Sometimes you can lose sight of the fact that both parties to the relationship have needs, feelings, histories, and varying abilities. It's easy also to fall into the trap of feeling that your partner should meet all of your wants and needs, all of the time. Remember the example in the last chapter about the husband who initially was willing to go with his wife to the ballet and to a play once in a while, but over time he increasingly became less willing to go, to the point of being downright unpleasant about it? That husband was not meeting her desire for a spouse who would enjoy the theater with her.

Maybe he could have tried to adjust his attitude, yes. But maybe, on the other hand, it just wasn't in him. Maybe she needed to let it go, as she eventually did. Think about your own wishes and expectations for your husband. What if you always wished that the two of you would go dancing every week, or take up long-distance biking, or explore new restaurants together, or work on household projects as a team? Whatever it is that you wished for or even expected that he would do for or with you that he isn't *actually* doing, sit down and think about why and how the failure to satisfy or please you is happening. Be fair in assessing whether your expectations are reasonable, and whether he is or is not capable, much less willing, to meet each and every one of your desires to your specifications.

It's Also Not All About Him

Many women have been raised in a household where the mother gave a great deal of deference to the father, so the tendency of these women is to do what was learned at their mother's knee. Even when a woman hasn't been raised in such a household, certain attitudes and expectations that are constantly conditioned into both women and men by the culture surrounding them can cause a marriage to be unfairly balanced in favor of the husband, even in this day and age.

Be wary of giving your husband too much responsibility, power, or credit. Despite how you might have learned to do things when you were a little girl, or what you see depicted on television or in movies, or even in advice articles in women's magazines, you should think for yourself about the proper dynamic between the two of you. Your husband is not your master. And he's also not your white knight who is supposed to take care of all of life's responsibilities or rescue you from every irresponsible thing you do. If your marriage does not work like a partnership, but instead feels more like a father-daughter relationship or a master-servant one, think about how this is playing out in your life and what you can do to change it.

Your Marriage Does Not Include The Advertising Industry

Honestly, I blame the media for a lot of the unreasonable expectations, failed hopes, and sense of entitlement or neglect that infects so many marriages today. How many of us feel slightly disgruntled when we see ads every holiday season showing happy consumers buying, buying, buying for their friends, family members, and lovers? How many of us feel just a little bit unloved when we see images of doting husbands bestowing their wives with gifts of flowers, chocolates, or jewelry every Valentine's Day, Mother's Day, and anniversary?

We know that weddings have gone the way of keeping-up-with-the-joneses insanity, with overwrought couples and their parents so often spending many tens of thousands of dollars for one day of celebration when they really cannot afford it. Now it seems life itself is being marketed to us, and very aggressively, as an unending stream of extravagant gift-giving and consumption. Don't fall prey to what the marketers are hyping to you as the life you should have. Should you really expect flowers every week, when it's a stretch to have the money for a dinner out? Should you expect your husband to surprise you with expensive jewelry every anniversary when you don't have a lot of excess discretionary funds in your budget? And frankly, is it reasonable to expect your husband to run around buying things for you given his personality, and yours? Some men have a really hard time with gift-giving, and it's not through a lack of love or caring. Some *women* make it hard for their husbands to buy gifts for them, because they're particular about what they wear and eat and what's used and shown in their home. Take all of these factors into consideration when deciding if your husband actually treats you well or not. Sure, you may wish that you could be that beautiful model in the ad who throws her head back in delight when her husband pulls up close to her and shows her the diamond necklace he just bought her, but if the reality of your life really doesn't allow for such extravagances, or if his style or yours really don't fit into that scenario, banish the notion from your expectations. Or at least, don't turn your "I wish" fantasy into a negative "my husband doesn't love or care for me enough" resentment.

It's hard in this culture to resist the temptation to jump on the consumer crazy train, but do rein yourself in – often – when you're forming your opinions about what your husband should do for you and spend on you.

The Realities of Day-To-Day Life

I've talked in earlier chapters about the importance of having a pre-marriage discussion about how you wish to live your lives day to day, but once it's happened, the discussion should be considered open-ended, not a closed case. Things do change. Jobs exert unanticipated pressures. Realities of babies and child raising don't match up to the fantasies one had in the beginning. From time to time, I urge you, do sit down and talk about how it's going. Are you happy with the amount of times you eat out in restaurants, bring in take-out to eat at home, or prepare home-cooked meals? Do you feel you're both being fair about who cleans up the kitchen every night, packs lunches, does the laundry, pays the bills? Is the house kept as clean as you would like, and are you sharing the work (or the cost) of that equitably? Are home repairs being tended to in a timely fashion? Do you wish your husband would do more of them himself, or agree to hire someone else to do some of the work in order to free up his time for fun stuff? Assess your situation, both to determine whether you're holding to your earlier agreements, and to consider whether some of those agreements need to be modified in light of life as it is today.

The Dreaded Facebook Version of Everyone Else's Life

We all know this but that doesn't mean that it doesn't bug us. Your friends, even those whom you love and hold dear, will brag and they will get to you. Sometimes they're simply joyous about something that's happening in their lives – a remodel, a trip, a new living room sofa, and they're really not intending to brag. That's OK, they're entitled, but maybe it hits a nerve anyway because you've been stressing over money and wondering whether you ever will be able to enjoy those same things yourself.

And sometimes people just brag for the sake of bragging. Facebook has made this a finely practiced art for many – and a winner-take-all, blood-soaked battlefield for a few. God help us when we're down and we see our friend's (or acquaintance's) *happy happy happy* photos of her fabulous trip to St. Martin, or we look at a glowing photo in our timeline of that perfect meal at that romantic candlelit restaurant that a friend is gushing about.

I've consigned some of these "my life is WAY better than yours" Facebook friends to an invisible status on my Facebook account by choosing "Hide from timeline" for their posts, and I urge you to do the same when you're relentlessly brought low by, but reluctant to unfriend, a relentless braggart. You still have the final say-so over whether she'll be allowed to push her oh-so-perfect life into your face every time you want to socialize online.

And my final words of wisdom regarding unreasonable expectations: The longer you live, I absolutely guarantee you, the more you'll learn that you never know what's going on behind others' doors. If you could only know what's happening behind the scenes, you'd be shocked more often than you think. Your neighbor with the diamond necklace may be living with a mountain of debt. Your friend whose husband gives her mushy cards at every turn might spend every night alone while he stays out with friends after work until midnight. That friend who's going on expensive vacations might be trying to prove to herself that her husband really loves her, despite the fact that he cheats on her repeatedly. The friend smiling widely as she holds up a glass of wine at dinner might have dragged along an unwilling husband who's utterly bored with her.

Don't let unreasonable expectations, advertising pressure, and the publicly shared version of everyone else's life throw you off balance. Keep looking at your husband as a human being, keep an eye on your own finances and what style of life makes sense for your own family, and, most of all, keep looking inside yourself and remembering your true values and real needs. Let those be your measure of happiness.

Research:

1. Margarita Tartakovsky, M.S. talks about the "7 Persistent Myths About Marriage." http://psychcentral.com/lib/7-persistent-myths-about-marriage/

2. Markus Steffen, Sue Klavans Simring, and Gene Busnar provide a humorous but blunt discussion of the common unrealistic expectations many people bring to marriage, in "Deflating Six Common Marriage Myths." http://www.dummies.com/how-to/content/deflating-six-common-marriage-myths.html They share this so-true quote: "The only thing perfect about marriage is the airbrushed wedding photo." - Anonymous

3. Francesca Di Meglio, Newlyweds Expert for About.com, offers some great tips on how to compromise in your new marriage. http://newlyweds.about.com/od/gettingalong/tp/How-To-Compromise.htm

4. "Whether it's movies or TV shows or pornography or pop songs, sometimes we get unrealistic expectations for what love and sex and relationships are supposed to be," director and actor Joseph Gordon-Levitt told *On Air with Ryan Seacrest* when being interviewed about his new movie, *Don Jon*. "And this is a comedy about that." http://www.ryanseacrest.com/2013/09/27/joseph-gordon-levitt-says-the-media-creates-unrealistic-expectations-for-relationships/#sthash.IbXZq32a.dpuf

Chapter 11

Nurture Yourself

The Down Side of Not Taking Care of Yourself

There's an invisible dividing line among women as they fully enter adulthood, and it's not who's prettiest or most popular or who's wealthy or not. It's more serious and more deep-seated, and it's totally up to the women themselves which side of the line they're going to live on.

The dividing line is between those who take care of themselves and those who don't.

It's so easy to fall on the "don't" side, especially if you're working full time and trying to further your career and raising children. You live in a world of "there's a purpose more important than just me" world, and much of your moral fiber may be telling you, over and over again, that you don't have time for… fill in the blank – getting to the gym, getting your hair done, preparing a healthy lunch for yourself, taking a bike ride, taking a day for yourself.

Life, as we adult women know, can be comprised of a series of deadlines, crises, and expectations piled on top of us from all directions.

Where in the instruction manual did it say that your needs and your health and your sanity don't count anymore?

One of the most powerful reflective exercises at a recent conference a friend of mine attended was when the participants, all women over 50, were asked to write a letter of advice to their former selves. The words of wisdom and of regret were heartfelt. "Don't forget yourself in your own life." "You are your own mother; love and take care of yourself as much as you do others." "Keep pursuing the things you love, even though you love and are responsible for others too." "Don't accept that anything 'has' to be a certain way. Walk away from the situation that's hurting you. It is not going to change, but you can."

If you operate out of a position of self-esteem, not self-sacrifice, you will be a stronger person, a happier person and, ultimately, a better performer as an employee, business person, professional, mother, or whatever it is that you're engaged in. And you will be enjoying your own life. I'm not saying you should neglect your children or fail to meet deadlines because you "have" to get to the gym seven days a week, but surely you can find an hour in your day to exercise, get fresh air, read, relax, or do something that makes you feel good about yourself.

You'd be surprised – or actually, maybe not – how many women feel they simply do not have a minute to spare, and so they forego any activity that doesn't have to do with their responsibilities to others. Once you get into this kind of grind, it's hard to see your way out, because if you don't have time to take a walk, ever, then where are you going to find the time to think about why you don't have any time to yourself, much less how to find it?

If you're in that rut, you're on the "don't" side of that dividing line between women who care for themselves and women who don't. And believe me, living on that side takes its toll – on your health, on your appearance, on your ability to assert yourself, on your happiness.

The stark fact is that if you don't attend to your needs and, yes, even your wants, you are more likely to gain weight, fall ill, suffer from depression, make mistakes, be irritable, complain, and suffer repeated blows to your ego when you find yourself poorly groomed or unfashionably dressed or you come up against instances when you can no longer do the things you used to love to do (dance, hike, kayak, play softball) because you've lost your skill or you're not fit enough anymore to do them.

Think about this in particular if you're in the midst of raising children right now: If you fail to take good care of yourself, it's not just that you put stress on your mind and body, causing many negative physical effects such as a weakened immune system, high blood pressure, depression, or anger management issues. It's also that you're having a direct and negative effect on your children. When you model unhealthy behavior, you're teaching your kids that taking care of themselves as they grow older is not important. And as a parent, your day-to-day performance of all that you do for your children can be compromised by your stress and fatigue and all of the ills that come with it. Parenting is hard enough. If you don't take care of yourself, you make it even harder.

With ill health and unhappiness a constant in your life, you very well may die younger too. And beyond the tragedy of that fact lies the irony that if you die earlier, you can't achieve the very things that you're sacrificing yourself in order to do; be there for your children, enjoy a long and memory-filled marriage, or achieve the pinnacle of your career success.

The Up Side of Caring For Yourself

If you take time for yourself and do things that you need and enjoy, you will gain clarity about all of the issues and responsibilities you're dealing with, making you more effective in the long run. And by time for yourself, I don't mean, necessarily, a day at the spa or a night out for yourself every week. I don't even necessarily mean a total getaway from everything you're responsible for. I know of one harried business owner and mother of two young children who just isn't comfortable leaving her children alone while she goes out on her own, and so she arranges a compromise getaway a couple of times per year for the whole family. She books a room at a lodge in the countryside in an area she loves that's surrounded by trees, walking trails, birds and wildlife. Just the place – its majestic natural beauty and the quiet and the clear air – fills her with happiness and a sense of calm. There is no schedule; just an expansive view of the hills and sky from their room, a wood-burning fireplace, the one on-premises restaurant, a pool surrounded by glass walls, and the outdoors.

This mom and businesswoman stops her work for 48 hours for this weekend. She isn't responsible to cook or decide where to go out to dinner or get anywhere at any given time. Her kids are happy to be in a whole new place wide open for adventure of their own making. There's very little expense, and there's no fighting over which place they're going to go or which ride they're going to take or toy or treat they're going to buy. And even her husband, with whom she's having a difficult relationship, is mellowed out by the natural surroundings.

"Without exception, I always have moments of peace and quiet during this weekend unlike in my daily life," she says, "and I always have a revelation somewhere along the way." On these weekends, she's realized how to solve a problem in one of the processes in her company's operation, or she's decided to correct an imbalance in a friendship that's been bugging her, or she's come to the conclusion that she needs to hire an accountant instead of continuing to personally prepare the joint tax return every year.

The weekends away aren't solitary or self-indulgent, but they're therapeutic and they give her perspective. I urge you to give yourself your own version of therapy in your life, whether it be a regular tai chi class or a weekly counseling session with a therapist or a weekend of camping with your family twice a year. It could even be as simple as taking a lunch hour by yourself on Mondays and Fridays to read a book in solitude. Whatever gives you a break from your everyday grind, do it and do it regularly, and tell yourself it's not selfish, it's self-loving and self-preserving. It helps not only you but ultimately all those to whom you owe duties and responsibilities.

Taking time for your own needs on a regular basis is an investment in serving all of the other people you care about. Time for yourself renews your energy, motivation, and capacity to deal with life – meaning you'll do more good for others over the long haul if you do more to take good care of yourself.

Is Your Husband Standing In The Way of Your Own Needs?

Often a married woman will get in the habit of not doing for herself because she doesn't want to make her husband feel that she doesn't want to be with him or do everything together as a couple. Keep in mind that if your husband has your best interests at heart, he won't begrudge the time you take out of your otherwise busy schedule to take care of yourself, your health, your friends, your hobbies, and your interests. Also bear in mind that the more you demonstrate your strength and independence, the more comforted he will be (or should be) knowing that while you love to have him around, you don't need him to be around every minute of the day and in every corner of your life.

There seems to be a misconception with some women that the more you deny yourself, the more your husband will know that you love him – and therefore he'll love you more. I don't think there is anything farther from the truth!

The Story of Ines

I have a client, Ines, who left her country, her mother and father, her family, friends and career to follow her then boyfriend to Miami, Florida. They got married and she worked tirelessly to help him grow his business, and she also went to school part time to finish her bachelor's degree. After 10 years, they had no children (in retrospect, a very lucky thing), and he decided he didn't want to be married anymore. He left their apartment with his belongings while she was at work, wiped out their bank accounts, and left her essentially penniless. The lease on their apartment was up and she couldn't afford to pay the next month's rent, much less ongoing rent and expenses. Fortunately, her sister had relocated to Miami and was able to help her until I filed papers for her and secured support from her husband, but the legal system was, as it always is, slow. For several months, she felt like a beggar while he was enjoying the fruits of their labor – his and hers.

Had Ines done more to take care of her needs – earning a degree and getting a job and establishing her own financial resources instead of halting her own plans or putting them on a slow schedule in order to concentrate only on his business success, she might have been in a much better position to go on and take care of herself when he decided to leave.

So How Are You Going to Take Care of Yourself?

What are some ways you can take better care of yourself than you've been doing? Think about these areas of your life, whether you've been selling yourself short, and how you can turn things around going forward.

Food

Take care with your own food. Make sure you're feeding yourself nutritious, high-quality food, whether this means dining out or doing more conscious food preparation at home. One downfall of many mothers of young children is to save time and trouble by eating what their children eat rather than what they prefer or know they themselves should be eating. They can start down this slippery slope by doing things such as preparing "mono meals" – macaroni and cheese and nothing else, for example, for finicky small children who don't do well when presented with too many food choices in one sitting. Rather than preparing her own sandwich or salad, for example, the mother might just – what the heck – eat that mac and cheese too when she's feeding her child – and maybe she eats too much of it because she's tired and bored and frustrated. As time goes on, she gets into the habit of feeding her kids what they won't object to, allowing the meals to veer toward easy and perhaps calorie-dense or less nutritious foods, and she continues to eat what she feeds them. If this is you, you might be able to reconfigure mealtime for your children, and for yourself. Maybe they're older now and you can make the meals more varied and nutritious, and still continue to prepare a single meal for all of you. Or maybe you can allow yourself to buy a few pre-made individual-serving salads at the market when shopping, and eat those at lunchtime. You'll be taking better care of yourself, and setting a better example for your children too at the same time.

The key to change is changing in small increments, consciously choosing to do things that are just a little different and easy to incorporate into the life that you're living now.

Don't do anything at all for a few hours every day – i.e., sleep!

It's surprising how many women in the "prime" of their lives are regularly sleep deprived. Sleep seems an easy thing to pare down in order to free up extra hours when you have so many things to do. But think of these reasons *not* to get by in life by denying yourself a full and adequate night's rest at the end of each day:

1. Sleep loss causes many traffic accidents; drowsiness can slow reaction time as much as being drunk. It can also be a major factor in other accidents and injuries on the job.
2. Loss of sleep impairs attention, alertness, concentration, reasoning, and problem solving.
3. Chronic sleep loss can increase your risk for heart disease, irregular heartbeat, high blood pressure, stroke, and diabetes.
4. According to sleep specialists, sleep-deprived men and women report lower libidos and less interest in sex.
5. When sleep deprivation is extended over time, it can contribute to depression. And while lack of sleep can worsen the symptoms of

depression, depression can then make it harder to fall asleep, feeding a vicious cycle.

6. Extended loss of sleep can lead to dull skin, fine lines, and dark circles under the eyes. When you don't get enough sleep, your body releases more of the stress hormone cortisol and too little of the human growth hormone that helps increase muscle mass, thicken skin, and strengthen bones.

7. Lack of sleep seems to increase the risk of obesity; according to a 2004 study, people who sleep less than six hours a day were almost 30 percent more likely to become obese than those who slept seven to nine hours. Among the common effects of sleep deprivation: increased cravings for high-fat, high-carbohydrate foods – another vicious cycle.

8. You could die, and I mean that quite literally. In the 1990's and early 2000's, British researchers studied sleep habits versus mortality among more than 10,000 British civil servants. Those who had cut their sleep from seven to five hours or fewer a night nearly doubled their risk of death from all causes, and in particular from cardiovascular disease.

Learn new ways to cope with stress

Try meditation. Try yoga. Try tai chi. Shut yourself in a room with a good book. Try soothing yourself with one of the adult coloring books that have become so popular.

Engage in exercise regularly

Join a gym, take a dance class, a yoga class or just take a walk. Do it for fun and for feeling good – not as another burdensome task.

Seek spiritual support

You might start participating in an organized religion, or take advantage of the counseling or group support offered by the church, synagogue, or mosque you already attend. Or find and join a support group, or research some self-help books that address the stress you're dealing with. Meditation is a most helpful tool.

Honor and nurture your own friendships

Sometimes your own friendships get minimized or pushed aside entirely, the more stressed you are. This is bad for you because it removes the most natural and comfortable source of support you have in your life. And it is actually, literally, bad for your physical as well as your psychological self. As Suzanne Braun Levine points out in her book *You Gotta Have Girlfriends*, "Girlfriends are also, it turns out, the keepers of each other's physical well-being. While researching *You Gotta Have Girlfriends* I found new studies of all kinds that showed how having girlfriends in your life reduces stress, enhances pleasure and even strengthens the immune system."

Take time alone, regularly

Enough said.

Engage in your hobbies and interests

What you enjoy doing is not what you should reject as frivolous or a waste of time. Enjoyment is good medicine, it's good food for your soul, and it's good for your continued strength and good will as you go about fulfilling all of your responsibilities in life.

Take a vacation already – at least once in a while

Go away from it all and have a vacation, one way or another, either alone or with female friends. It could be anything from a no-cost weekend visiting a friend to a long weekend in wine country – whatever is possible and gives you time to renew.

Research:

1. The classic example of women not taking care of their own needs is the "do-it-all mom." Kavita Varma-White talks about this trend on *TODAY*: "In 'doing it all,' moms neglect an important person: themselves." http://www.today.com/news/doing-it-all-moms-neglect-important-person-themselves-2D11899303
2. "Self Care for Parents," published by SCAN, building help for children and families in Northern Virginia, talks about the deleterious effects of a parent's poor self-care on the lives of their children. https://www.scanva.org/support-for-parents/parent-

resource-center-2/self-care-for-parents/

3. *WebMD* has published an eye-opening article by Camille Peri on the dangers of sleep deprivation, "Coping With Excessive Sleepiness: 10 Things to Hate About Sleep Loss." http://www.webmd.com/sleep-disorders/excessive-sleepiness-10/10-results-sleep-loss

4. Suzanne Scurlock-Durana offers a very do-able set of guidelines on taking good care of yourself in "Nurture Yourself from Moment to Moment - How to listen to your body and give it what it needs." http://life.gaiam.com/article/nurture-yourself-moment-moment

5. On the *Kris Carr* blog, "home of the crazy sexy wellness revolution," guest blogger Tama J. Kieves shares "How to Nurture Yourself & Be Your Own Mother." http://kriscarr.com/blog/how-to-nurture-yourself-be-your-own-mother/

6. "You Gotta Have Girlfriends; A Post-50 Posse Is Good For Your Health," by Suzanne Braun Levine. http://www.huffingtonpost.com/suzanne-braun-levine/health-benefits-of-friends_b_3087957.html

Chapter 12
Authenticity & Reality

It's a conundrum, perhaps; doing all that you can to make your marriage work, and at the same time trying to evaluate whether it's worth it to keep your marriage going. But honest assessments are essential. Here are some questions to ask, not just now, but every few years:

How do you feel, overall, most of the time? Happy? Angry? Frustrated? Sad? Disappointed? Neutral? Bored? Like you have a partner at your side? Or like you're going it alone?

Look At Yourself Honestly

In looking at your feelings, try to be honest with yourself about how you feel, how intense your feelings are, and what is causing those feelings. Try to separate those elements of your mood that come from within, and those that come from external causes. Perhaps you've suffered from depression all of your life, for example. The difficulty with acknowledging and treating depression is that often, the things going on in your life are legitimate causes of unhappiness. But maybe you've always had a tendency to experience more intense episodes of deep unhappiness than the circumstances warrant – or you simply don't have a good arsenal of coping skills to deal with difficult situations. Maybe your tendency toward depression is coloring your overall sense of happiness or frustration or disappointment. Try to look at your whole life in comparison to your married life and determine how much of your sense of wellness – or not – might be coming from roots in your own personality.

On the flip side, take some time to examine those areas where you might be tolerating a bad situation but you've spent your whole married life explaining away why it's necessary to do so. "My husband is trying really hard to make it up the corporate ladder, so he has to stay late at the office all the time, entertain clients, and travel whenever his boss tells him to. I hate what it does to our marriage having him gone all the time, but it's for a good reason."

Is it though? Perhaps you were willing to accept the long hours and time away in the beginning when you envisioned rewards and riches coming your way in the future – but maybe your acceptance has become institutionalized in your marriage far beyond the time period when it was appropriate. What was the deal when you agreed, explicitly or implicitly, to such a life? That it would go on for only a few years – but now it's been ten years and the demands on his personal and family time still haven't let up? Or that your husband would earn so much money down the line that you'd have the financial means to send your children to the best schools, live in a beautiful home, and take dream vacations – only those riches haven't materialized and all you're getting in exchange for a semi-single life is enough money to pay the bills? Take a fresh look at the "givens" you've agreed to or allowed to become a part of your marriage, and consider whether they're appropriate or tolerable today.

Be honest with yourself. Are the late nights legitimately work related? Is his travel always necessary? Are you turning a blind eye toward his behavior because you have been trapped in the golden cage?

Who are you today, compared to who you were when you got married? Have you changed in outlook, goals, beliefs, values? People do change, some evolve and grow and sometimes the change can wreak havoc in their relationships. And sometimes, people tried to change for a time in order to fit themselves into a life they envisioned, only to find years later that they can't keep up the ruse anymore and they're tired of pretending to be someone they're not.

What if you originally thought that you'd gladly stay home to raise your children, thinking that life would be picture-perfect, only you've felt a growing dissatisfaction the longer you've been away from your career? Or what if you thought you'd execute a well-planned sequence of events in which you gave birth to your babies, took your maternity leave, and then returned immediately to your career path, only now you find that you'd much rather raise your children yourself and not work?

What if you earned a professional degree and started out on a traditional career path, but you've felt a growing urge to start your own business?

What if you agreed to live in an area of the country thinking it was best for your family but you've actually never been able to feel comfortable where you are, and you feel more strongly every year that you'd rather live elsewhere?

What if you've tried to go the housewife route and you just flat-out aren't happy in that role, despite your early conviction to be the best at-home wife and mother that you could be?

Who Is Your Spouse Today – Compared To Who He Was Before?

Time and circumstance change everyone – sometimes a little, sometimes a lot. Has your husband changed? In what ways? Has he developed habits that accommodate your particular quirks and needs? Or has he developed ways of doing things that seem intended to annoy or thwart you? Is he kind to you, or does he insult you or belittle you? Does he share his thoughts and concerns with you, his plans and dreams, or has he closed down the lines of communication with you over time? Do you still laugh together? Does he support you or drain you?

Do you still like him? Does he treat you fairly, carry his weight when it comes to the finances, home and the children? Does he listen to you, pay attention to your needs, say that he loves you once in a while?

You may be coming at these questions from a position of quiet blindness to an array of ways that he mistreats you and that you've explained away for years. Or you may be feeling a seething anger toward him that you can barely contain. Try to start over, to go back to the beginning and look at him from as neutral a stance as you can, and from your own position of self-respect. Imagine that you're not married, and you're getting to know this man. Do you like how he is – especially how he behaves toward you and toward your children? Or is his behavior bordering on apathetic, cruel or neglectful, so much so that you would never consider marrying him if he were a new person in your life?

If there are problems, disappointments, or causes for anger, try to list them separately, under categories that make sense to you. Under each category, describe some actual events that caused your feelings of unhappiness. Make your list and your explanations as concrete as you can. Now leave it all for a while. Come back to visit it later, at a different time and when you're in a different mood. Do you see the same problems and feel the same feelings still? If so, there's work to be done, and at least now you've got a roadmap to go by that you can use in talking with him or with a counselor or advisor.

If There Have Been Changes, Are They For Better Or For Worse?

Sometimes major upheavals in a marriage turn out to be good for both of you. Maybe you started out as a gung-ho career woman but you've decided to stay home with the children, and you're very happy with your decision. If your husband is happy too, congratulations on successfully navigating a major change in your relationship.

But sometimes major changes can be disastrous, and not necessarily through either spouse's fault.

One divorce I handled – a very contentious and extended legal battle, unfortunately – happened largely because the wife made a major change in her life that ended up sinking the marriage. It wasn't her fault, and in a way it wasn't her husband's fault either. She started out working in a traditional job, and then got pregnant. She planned to take maternity leave and return to work. But unfortunately, she lost her first baby to pre-term birth, and she was changed forever by the loss. After her baby died, she could not imagine having a baby and leaving it with a caregiver while she worked full-time. She decided to stay home when she had her next baby, and her husband willingly agreed with her. He'd been changed by the loss too.

However, my client's quite intense feelings about wanting to be with her baby didn't entirely jive with her innate personality, which was career oriented. After a few years she had two small children at home and she found she wanted to be working again, partly because it was in her nature, and partly because her husband had started to treat her like "the little wife" to whom he gave orders. She wanted to earn an income again, and she wanted to put balance back into her relationship with her husband. But she didn't want to go to work for an employer, placing her under the control of a boss who could dictate when and where she must work, whether she must leave home to travel, and when she could take time off. She decided to start her own business instead, a parenting magazine, which she could run from her home.

Her husband was less than thrilled with this idea, and said so, but his resistance didn't make sense at all to my client at the time. Why shouldn't she run her own business? She was smart, she was a hard-worker, she had a background in publishing. So she forged ahead, figuring that it would all work out when her magazine was a success and her husband could see that his lack of faith in her was ill-founded.

In a word, it went to hell from there. The key problem was that the wife did not really understand why her husband objected to her plans, and she made her own conclusions about the basis for his misgivings and her ability to do away with them by proving that he was wrong to doubt her. What she failed to see – and really couldn't have known without some real discussion around the issue – was that her husband had absolutely no experience within his own upbringing with successful entrepreneurialism, and he was terrified by the whole idea. His father had worked for the government. His mother had been a housewife and later on in life worked as a low-level secretary at a large company.

The only person he'd known in his life to try to run a business was an uncle who had started his own enterprise and then gone bankrupt. The husband had grown up hearing many discussions about the disaster that his uncle had made of his life and of his family's. From that experience he had formed very strong, fearful feelings about the foolhardiness of setting off on a business idea of your own creation, believing that anyone who tried to run a business of his own was going to ruin his family financially.

Meanwhile the wife, a strong personality, smart, and a go-getter all her life, was bound and determined that her husband was not going to tell her what she could or could not do. She had to put a stop to his growing practice of treating her dismissively and disrespectfully. She had to make him treat her like an equal again.

So instead of either the husband or wife realizing the depth of the other's feelings, the two of them set out unwittingly upon a path of pain and destruction. She wrote a business plan but did not get assistance with it because he refused to look at it and he balked at the idea of "wasting money" on a consultant to help her. She took her plan to the bank and applied for a business loan but found that the bank would not loan her the money without her husband's co-signature, since he was a wage earner and she, because of her decision to stay home with her children, had not earned an income for five years. Her husband refused to co-sign on the loan.

Determined to keep her husband from standing in her way, and sure of her ability to make a go of her plan, she forged ahead without the funding, trying to do everything for the business herself without a staff or hired help of any sort. She was chief, cook, and bottle washer.

At the same time, her husband not only did not step in to help at home or with the children, he took every chance he could get to take offense at any sign that she was falling down on the job as a homemaker or mother. If there were dishes in the sink when he came home, he was furious. If she stayed up late to get work done, he fumed. If she asked him to drive the children to a playdate or a doctor's appointment, he refused, saying he couldn't afford to ask for any special favors at work such as leaving a half hour early, because thanks to her risky behavior in starting her business, he had to protect his job at all costs. He refused to share any household chores of any sort, saying angrily that he worked hard enough as it is, and if she didn't have her "stupid business," she'd have time to do all of those chores herself. Over time he began actively sabotaging her and adding to the sense of chaos and ruin; when she co-hosted the launch of an annual event with the mayor of their city, he refused to attend, much less take the children to witness it, and he kept the television off at home that afternoon and told the children only that "Mom can't stay home with you because she has to run off for her stupid magazine." He started leaving his bath towels on the floor, dishes around the house, clothes strewn about the bedroom. He shouted at the children when they didn't throw a ball correctly, address him as "sir," or want to go on a walk with him, saying that they were spoiled and lazy and their mom was ruining them. Often on a weekend day he'd get in his truck and drive off without a word of explanation.

Imagine this scenario playing out over several years, which it did. By the time my client threw in the towel, her husband had convinced the children that their mother was neglectful and selfish and that they lived in the worst house on the block. Meanwhile the business had accumulated some significant debt, and her husband was spending any free time he had helping out a co-worker, a young woman thirteen years younger than my client, with *her* household chores, because she was going through a divorce and "needed his help."

The anger, recriminations, complicated financial and personal affairs, and damage that had been done by the time my client came to me were a real tragedy. And if you go back to the very beginning of this couple's tale, the initial changes that ultimately led to their downfall were really neither person's fault. It's so tragic that neither of them took the time to step back and evaluate what was going on, and try to change their path of destruction.

Have You Been Growing Up Or Growing Stale?

Over the time that you've been married, have you learned and grown? Have you come to understand your husband better than you did when you married? Have you developed better communication skills so that when there are problems or misunderstandings, you're able to get through them with less difficulty than you had in the beginning?

Do you feel that you've learned as you've gone along – about your husband, about yourself, about what a marriage is and can be, and about life in general? Or does your history together feel more like a series of calamities interspersed with boredom? Do your arguments seem to simply dredge up the same old complaints and end in a stand-off every time?

Of course no marriage is going to feel the same after ten years as it did in the beginning, and in some ways there is always loss, but that's not necessarily a sign that things are going in a bad direction. Your initial passion and excitement simply cannot be sustained, for example – no one's can. But your friendship can and should deepen. Your ability, and his, to accept those less-than-endearing traits you each have should mellow. You should be building memories that can be treasured as life goes on. Are these hallmarks of your marriage? If not, be honest when you consider whether you'd like things to go on just as they are.

In Chapter 11, I mentioned an exercises at a conference for women over 50 in which the women were asked to write a letter of advice to their former selves. This is something I suggest you do now, especially if you feel that things are not going so well for you and your husband. Who were you back before the two of you got married? What were your dreams then? What was your vision of how your life was going to be? Think about how that person felt – the young woman who had her whole life and all of her hopes before her. Was she thinking intelligently back then or should she have been more realistic? Was she blind to the problems that were going to inevitably come across her path if she married the man who is now your husband? Should she have stood her ground at important points of decision making? Should she have stated her feelings more clearly, stood up for what she believed in or wanted out of life? Write a letter of advice to her. Be specific about some of the "what ifs" that that young woman couldn't have seen back then but that you, the older and wiser woman that you are, can foresee coming her way, and advise her on how to make wise choices and take positive actions.

Now set the letter aside (as you did with your list of problems earlier) and revisit it later. Try to read the letter as if you're now twenty years older than you are, and you've done nothing to correct the problems or pitfalls that you've discussed in the letter. How does that make you feel? Like you weathered the storm and you're glad of it; that it was worth it for the sake of the marriage? Or like you just threw away twenty years of the life you wanted for yourself in exchange for a life that is full of disappointment and regret?

What Now?

Now that you've done all of this work reflecting on yourself, your husband, your relationship, and the quality and direction of your life, what now? If your marriage is not what you expected it would be, should you adjust your expectations to be more realistic, or is it time to admit to yourself that this marriage is not what you want for your life?

Of course this is not an easy question to answer, but you are the only person responsible for your own life and your own happiness, so answer it you must. Think about the time that's gone by. Think about the years to come. Think about your children. Even think about your husband's chances for his own happiness going forward in life. Would the two of you be better apart? Are there so many problems and so few reasons to continue trying to make a go of it that the situation is beyond repair?

If so, what now?

Research:

1. "10 Ways To Tell If Your Marriage Is Over," by Drs. Evelyn and Paul Moschetta. http://www.yourtango.com/experts/drs-evelyn-and-paul-moschetta/10-ways-tell-if-your-marriage-heading-divorce

2. *The Stir* has an eye-opening slideshow that shows quite visually those clarifying questions that can help you decide if your marriage is truly over. http://thestir.cafemom.com/love_sex/173604/5_Signs_Your_Marriage_Is

3. Cathy Meyer, divorce support expert on About.com, lists the "Top 7 Warning Signs Your Marriage May End in Divorce ." http://divorcesupport.about.com/od/signsyourmarriageisover/tp/warningsigns.htm

PART THREE

Calling it Quits: Living "Reasonably" Ever After - Separation & Divorce

Chapter 13

Preparation

Yes, it may be unthinkable, but don't allow yourself to be paralyzed by fear or shame if divorce is looming on the horizon. The time to take action is now when you're first thinking about it, or as soon as you suspect that your spouse is.

Maybe it won't happen, maybe it will, but you'd be a fool not to prepare for the worst. When one country suspects that its neighbor is arming for war, do its leaders pretend that nothing is happening and hope for the best? No, they alert their department heads, their legislature, their armed forces. They step up their surveillance. They position their army, navy, and air force, stockpile weapons, add security to their borders. If the situation worsens, they may begin preparing the public for the inevitable, and reaching out to other nations for backup and support.

You should begin the same process. You don't have to declare war today. But prepare for it in case it happens tomorrow.

It's been said that most men who are thinking about divorce start planning up to two years in advance to secure their finances. Know this as true – and use this knowledge to protect yourself. Take a look at the following list prepared by a forensic accountant for the Women's Institute for Financial Education, of the ways husbands often hide money when they're preparing for a divorce:

- Antiques, artwork or hobby equipment that is overlooked and undervalued. Also look for these items plus new or expensive furnishings in his office.
- Collusion with his employer to delay payment of bonuses, stock options or raises until after the divorce.
- Income, often cash that is unreported on tax returns and financial statements. What you spent money on during marriage might well have exceeded reported

income, so document your cash expenditures.

- A custodial account set up in the name of a child, using the child's social security number.
- "Debt repayment" of a phony debt to a friend or family member, with the pre-arrangement that the friend will hold the money until after the divorce, then give it back to your husband.
- Salary paid to a straw man, i.e. nonexistent employee of your husband's business. The checks will be voided after divorce.
- Money paid from the business to someone close, such as a father or girlfriend, for business services not rendered. As with the phony debt repayment, the money will be held until the divorce is final, then given back to your spouse.
- Delay in signing long-term business contracts until after the divorce.
- Expenses paid for a girlfriend, such as gifts, travel, jewelry, rent, or college tuition.
- Investment in municipal bonds or Series EE Savings Bonds for which no interest is reported on tax returns.
- Bank statement that suddenly stop arriving at home.
- The annual bonus that suddenly does not materialize; his salary suddenly dropping.
- His attitude becoming secretive, defensive, or controlling about money, which may be a cover for dissipating assets and diverting income.

Pull Yourself Together – Now

Knowing what your husband could be doing with the family's money – and believe me, if he's thinking of divorcing you, he probably *is* employing at least some of the tactics listed above to hide money from you – it's clear that you need to pull yourself together and take action to protect yourself right now. Work through the list below, as quickly and as efficiently as you can.

1. Get together a list of all known bank accounts, and their balances. Note which are joint and which are solely owned by you or by him. Make a chart that is well-organized to record this information, with

columns for banking institution, exact account name, ownership, account number, and bank routing number. Include columns to show the balance in each account today, last month, and three months, six months, nine months, and a year ago.

2. Make a list of all known investments and their values, organizing this information in chart form as well, including name of the investment institution, ownership, account number, and value of the investment.

3. Make copies of your spouse's recent pay stubs. If you can, also make copies of older pay stubs; one every six months going back the last two years.

4. Make copies of the titles to your cars. Also make copies of the purchase documents or note the dates you purchased your cars, the purchase prices, and the mileage and condition of each car.

5. Copy the deed to your home. Note the date purchased and the purchase price, and make copies of all records of improvements to the home such as additions, remodels, window replacements, upgrades to heating or cooling systems, and new landscaping.

6. Look at recent sales prices of similar homes in your area, and use that information to determine the approximate value of your home. If you need help with this, you can ask a real estate broker for some assistance (but do ask him or her to keep your conversation confidential), or ask your banker for a reputable appraiser.

7. Make a list of your possessions, including your jewelry. Document this list with photographs. If you have receipts for the purchases, make copies of those too.

8. Run a credit check to see what debts and liabilities are showing up on your record. Refer to Chapter 7 for information on how and where to obtain credit reports.

Make Plans To Bring It Out In The Open

If you're going to divorce, you have to tell people and make some initial decisions. You can do this. Sure, your heart and your fear may be telling you that you can't possibly pull your thoughts together or know what to do next, but your brain knows better. Instead of wringing your hands and asking yourself "What will I do?", sit down with a pad and pen or your laptop and start a the top of the page with the title "What I *Will* Do." You may not be able to foretell the future, but you *can* start with the questions of how you will make the divorce known to your family, friends, boss, colleagues, and most important, to your children.

If you and your husband are talking openly and rationally with one another about ending your marriage, then discuss how you will tell people and when and where. But if you're not working cooperatively on the divorce or if there's great acrimony between you, then write down for yourself how you will handle as best you can the unpleasant task of letting everyone know what's happening.

Consider and decide upon the following:

How will you tell the children?

This is a highly individual decision, but you may want to consult with a friend who's been through it before, or a child psychologist who can give you advice specific for the ages of your children. Think about when and where and under what circumstances you'll tell your kids. It's worth sitting down and practicing what you will say, too. Children will always remember vividly the day they found out their parents were divorcing, so do it with compassion.

In formulating a plan for telling the children, determine ahead of time what decisions concerning your children will be made by you and your husband, or you alone, and what decisions will include their input. Come up with answers ahead of time for some very likely questions: Where are we going to live? Will we ever see Daddy again? Are we going away? Are we going to be poor? Do you have a boyfriend? Does Daddy have a girlfriend? Why don't you love each other anymore?

In thinking about how you will answer these questions if they're asked, be very, very aware of what's too much and what's too little information. Avoid saying anything that sounds like blame or rancor toward your husband, no matter how you might really feel inside. Be reassuring, but be truthful. Admit that you're sad, but tell them that you believe that you will be happy later. Allow them to say what they feel, but put a lid on it if the discussion seems to be heading out of control. In short – be the best parent that you can be in this most painful and life-altering moment for your children.

How will you tell your own family and your in-laws?

With regard to your own family members, much will depend of course on what kind of relationship you have with each family member. Do try to exercise as much maturity and restraint as you can muster. Do realize that your family will need some reassuring too. They love you and they will understandably worry about how you're going to weather the whole ordeal. Be prepared to answer some questions about preliminary information ("Has he moved out?" "Do you have a lawyer?") but also be prepared to firmly close the discussion if the questions become too probing or inappropriate. You don't owe anyone entry into the most intimate details of your marriage, nor should you overshare even if you're tempted to vent now that you've finally let the cat out of the bag. I'm not saying that you need to act the parent even when dealing with your own siblings or mother, but do realize how very deeply what you are telling them may affect them. And remember that for your children's sake, you should do what you can to preserve and protect your soon-to-be ex-husband's standing in the eyes of your family. All within reason, of course. If your husband was flaunting his affair with his secretary, wiped out all of your accounts, trashed you on Facebook, and left you with creditors banging on the door, there's not much you can – or should feel obligated to do – to maintain anyone's respect for him.

With regard to telling your in-laws, in my opinion it's best for each spouse to tell his or her own parents, sisters, and brothers. But don't act as though you don't have a right to communicate with them as well. They're automatically placed into an awkward position by the impending divorce. They are your children's family too, though, and you should try to maintain some level of communication with them, and let them know that you still value your relationship with them (if you do) even though their son/brother and you are getting a divorce.

How will you tell your friends?

If you have close friends, most likely they already know what's going on. You might do them the courtesy of telling them, though, when you've made the divorce public so they know that others are aware now too. With regard to less close friends and acquaintances, no need to make a big announcement; just share the fact of the divorce whenever it makes sense when you have a conversation with anyone you know.

How will you tell your boss and colleagues?

Your boss needs to know as soon as you know that events may have an impact on your performance as an employee. Do your boss the courtesy of giving him or her as much advance notice as possible so that plans can be made ahead of time to cover you when you must attend meetings or go to court. The earlier you inform the boss, the more you will show yourself to be a level-headed and committed employee who can be trusted to uphold her responsibilities no matter what else is going on in her life.

With regard to your colleagues, this is a murky area influenced by a lot of factors. Is your office big or small? Cozy and friendly or strictly business? Is the atmosphere gossipy, or do most people refrain from talking about others behind their backs? Play out how you share the news in a way that will minimize the whispering and speculation and show you to be the same self-respecting and confident colleague you've always been.

Making It Official; Serving Papers

The act of serving papers, or being served, can cause a wave of anger, grief, loss, or even shock to wash over you, even though you knew it was going to happen. If you're serving the papers, decide when, where, and how you will accomplish it. If you're having another person make the service, dictate how and where to do it in order to minimize disruptions as much as possible. And if you know you're going to be served soon, prepare yourself emotionally now. I would advise you to hire a lawyer in preparation, before you've been given the actual notice of divorce. Your lawyer can help you get your ducks in a row so you're prepared as well as you can be for the ordeal you're about to go through. If you're served papers at work or with the children or in a public place, remain as calm as possible and save your close reading of the document and your reactions for the time when you can be alone.

It is possible to accept service of divorce papers without the formality of a process server knocking aggressively at your door. And most attorneys can and will accept service on your behalf or on behalf of your husband (if you are the initial filer). I prefer this method because it sets the tone for an amicable process, even if the peace doesn't last.

Who Will Stay And Who Will Go?

Of course the first decision that will have to be made when a divorce is put into motion, is who will stay in the marital home and who will move out. It's not always so easy to decide. You might be in a situation where your husband is so furious and so unreasonable and willing to fight to the death over every single decision, that you decide it's easier to simply move out and find a new place of your own for the time being, fair or not. This would be especially true if he's irrational and you fear for your safety or the well-being or safety of your children. But in most cases, you should plan to be the one who stays, and be prepared to insist on it if your husband resists. Why? Because it's difficult to separate all of your possessions in one fell swoop; if you're the one to move out, chances are you'll leave quite a bit behind, figuring you'll sort things out later. Can your husband be trusted to maintain joint possessions and also those that are yours alone, until the final division of property takes place?

Then there's the issue of leverage. If you move out and leave the house to your husband, he gets to stay put in the home he's always known; no need to file a change of address, open new utility accounts, or get to know a new set of neighbors. He's set, he's enjoying exclusive use of the home that the two of you have put money and sweat into, and his motivation for getting things settled, which may include the need to sell the home and divide the proceeds, has drained away.

Finally there's the potential impact of moving out on the ultimate custody of your children. If you're thinking about possibly moving out on your own, leaving your children and your husband in the family home, consider what attorney Judith L. Poller said in an article in *Forbes*: "If either party leaves, that may affect his/her claims of wanting to be the custodial parent. Until there is a parenting plan in place, if the parties are interested in maintaining a meaningful relationship in the child's life, 'abandonment' prior to an agreement being entered into, may indicate a lack of real interest in the child's daily life." That's a very scary thought. But remember that it is highly unlikely that moving out would affect your rights to your children these days. Some states have written the word "custody" out of their statutes and replaced them with the notions of timesharing and parental responsibility. If your position will be that the other parent is not a fit parent, it may not bode well for you if you left your children in the home, even if temporarily. Unlikely though it may be that your claim for timesharing with your children and parental responsibility would be weakened by moving out of the home, think it through.

Research:

1. *Divorce 360* has published a very useful checklist to follow if you're headed for divorce – or even if you aren't sure yet, but you think you are: "Deciding Checklist: Should You Stay in Marriage? Here's What To Do (and what not to do)." http://www.divorce360.com/divorce-articles/counseling/save-marriage/deciding-checklist-should-you-stay-in-marriage.aspx?art id=357&page=2_

2. "Where to Search for Hidden Assets During Divorce," by Candace Bahr, CEA, CDFA and Ginita Wall, CPA, CFP®. http://www.wife.org/ss-hiddenassets.htm

3. Perhaps the worst moment in the entire process of divorce is telling the children. *Parent Magazine* offers good advice in "How to Tell Your Kids That You're Getting a Divorce," by Jeannette Moninger. http://www.parents.com/parenting/divorce/children/how-to-tell-your-kids-that-you-are-getting-a-divorce/

4. Elizabeth Shaw of *iVillage* has written a lovely overview (if "lovely" is a term that can be used here) on what it will be like going through a divorce. Her article, "Nine Things No One Tells You About Getting a Divorce" is published on, of all things, *eHarmony.* http://www.eharmony.com/dating-advice/about-you/nine-things-no-one-tells-you-about-getting-a-divorce/#.VbLl DvlVhBc

5. HG.org offers four practical tips on what to do after you've been served divorce papers, in "Four Tips after Being Served Divorce Papers." http://www.hg.org/article.asp?id=24481

6. LawHelp.org offers a comprehensive Q & A on how to serve divorce papers on your spouse, at http://www.lawhelp.org/dc/resource/serving-the-divorce-papers-on-your-spouse?ref=IjGd3

7. "Should You Move Out Of The Marital Home? Learn From Divorce Attorneys, Not The Tabloids." http://www.forbes.com/sites/jefflanders/2013/06/11/should-you-move-out-of-the-marital-home-learn-from-divorce-attorneys-not-the-tabloids/#79290a325a52

Chapter 14
Legal Counsel

If you had a heart attack, you wouldn't go to an orthopedist, right? When you have questions relating to divorce or separation, child custody issues, etc., I strongly urge you to seek counsel who focuses on family and matrimonial law.

It's important to get legal counsel and financial guidance before you make any decisions – even the most preliminary. Face that fact now – don't try to wing it until things get really messy. Who you hire to represent and guide you is truly the most important part of the whole process of divorce, and the earlier you find your counsel and advisor, the more smoothly things are apt to go.

How To Find The Right Lawyer

The lawyers involved will make all the difference! This has been proven again and again. So how do you find a lawyer who will understand you and do the very best job to protect you? Word of mouth can be a good resource. Do you know someone else who's been through a divorce recently and was happy with her lawyer? That's one place to start. But be careful about who you ask; the best advice for you will come from another person who's much like you in personality and outlook. So if you have a friend who seemed to relish sticking it to her husband every way she could while she was going through her divorce, but that's not your style, then don't ask her what attorney she used. Chances are the lawyer who was a good match for her will not be a good match for you.

There are others you can ask too. Professionals in other areas often know of divorce lawyers and the reputations they've earned. Ask your financial advisor, your therapist, attorneys you know who practice in other areas, or any CPAs you're acquainted with. You can get some excellent leads on lawyers, and maybe some information about their backgrounds and style of work, from these sources.

Finally there are many online directories that list attorneys by geographic location and area of practice, and some also provide information on the lawyers' performance such as rankings and disciplinary actions. Lawyers.com is one such source that is searchable by state and specialty, and includes each lawyer's Martindale-Hubbell® Peer Review Ratings™ along with client reviews. Findlaw.com is another source; it includes attorney listings by city and practice area, and also has a handy list of links to disciplinary boards by state. You can click through to your state board's website and research an attorney you're considering, to see if there are any negative notations on his or her record.

A Financial Advisor Is Essential Too

Much if not most of the issues to be settled in every divorce have to do with money and property. When you're in the midst of a divorce, you're embroiled in what may be the biggest financial negotiation of your life. You need a financial advisor at your side, because there are so many factors to consider above and beyond "how much is there, and how do we divide it." There are tax considerations; risk factors inherent in various types of investments or financial instruments; potential for growth or loss; estate planning issues; questions of division of assets versus sale of assets and division of proceeds, and other factors. Unless you're a financial advisor yourself, you are not likely to understand or even know what financial issues face you – and even if you *are* a financial advisor, I would urge you nevertheless to retain the services of another advisor to assist you. A separate set of eyes, experience, and outlook are invaluable.

When a case centers around alimony and the division of assets and liabilities, the lawyers involved will hire forensic accountants for you. The parties can agree to a neutral accountant, who essentially works for both sides, or each party can have his and her own. This can result in dueling experts at trial and of course, double the expense, but some cases require it.

You may want your own personal accountant or financial advisor. The process of finding a financial advisor is much like the process of finding a good lawyer. Ask those you know who have used financial advisors and recommend them highly. Talk to lawyers in any area of law, and therapists and CPAs. And consult online resources that can provide helpful information on credentials, years of experience, client reviews, and information on any disciplinary or other negative actions. At the very least, make sure that any financial advisor you work with has the "certified financial planner," or CFP, designation. The Certified Financial Planner Board of Standards allows you to search for CFP certificants on its website.

What About Using a Mediator Instead of Going to Court?

Your spouse may suggest using a mediator instead of filing a divorce action in court, or others might have advised you to do so in order to minimize the cost and the litigious nature of the process. This may or may not be good advice for you. Here are some things to consider:

First, try to find a mediator certified in family law and know that a mediator is not a substitute for a lawyer, but rather is a possible alternative to formal court proceedings. A mediator will act as a neutral third party who meets with both parties to the divorce and their attorneys to assist them in negotiating a resolution to their divorce. Unlike judges or arbitrators, mediators do not render decisions that are binding on the parties to the divorce, so it is possible to go through the mediation process and come out of it *without* a divorce settlement agreement, in which case you will then be faced with the prospect of filing papers and starting the whole formal process in court. That said, in most cases mediation does end successfully with a divorce agreement acceptable to both parties, and the more lengthy and expensive process of conducting divorce proceedings through the court system will have been avoided. A mediator cannot advise you on whether you are making a good deal or not, the way your lawyer will analyze your case and the outcome.

So let's assume you want to proceed with mediation. Do your homework before agreeing to a particular mediator to handle your case. Make sure the mediator you use has a good track record. Find out how many couples he or she has worked with and what percentage settled. Once a potential mediator has made the cut, then compare price, length of time the process is likely to take, personality, and style of the mediator before you decide. Family law mediations can go on for hours, way past 5 pm, so plan accordingly.

Paying For Your Lawyer And Advisors

Divorce lawyers do not work on contingency fees; they are paid set hourly rates for their services, as are financial advisors and mediators (should you choose to go the mediation route). How are you going to pay for all of that?

The simple answer is that you must find the money somewhere because you need the training and expertise of the best people in their fields in order to protect your interests and make sure you get all that you're entitled to. Chances are you'll end up with a better settlement, a better plan for your children and possibly more money, if you're represented well during your divorce than if you try to save money by going with less than the best lawyer and advisors or, worse, you try going it alone.

Be creative and don't be too prideful when you're searching out and considering the resources available to you. Your own parents might be willing to help out with expenses until the process is over. Or you might be able to sell an asset or cash out an account to free up the funds needed. A friend, sister, brother, or cousin might be willing to loan you the money until your settlement comes through.

It may be uncomfortable to ask for help, but don't be afraid to do so. Remember, you're protecting your own future and financial stability right now, and that of your children too if you have them, and in the long run that helps you avoid becoming a burden to your parents, friends, or siblings because you'll be able to take care of yourself when this divorce is completed. You can even be a support for others in need, once your divorce is settled fairly. As with a car repair, you may wish that you your car didn't break down and you didn't have the expense you're facing now, but you know that it's something that you must pay for anyway if you want to drive your car again and do so safely.

Before you ask for money or sell an asset or even begin writing checks, sit down and do a budget – and thank yourself for your skills in budget-making if you followed my advice back in Chapter 5. Talk first with your attorney and financial advisor and come up with a reasonable estimate of what this whole process is going to cost you, and the time period during which the expenses will be paid out. Understand that whom your spouse hires will make a big difference in the way the litigation plays out. You and your attorney may want to be reasonable, but some lawyers churn their files – and even frivolous motions require a response. This makes it difficult for your lawyer to estimate your total fees and costs.

See how much of those expenses, if any, might come out of your existing cash flow. Determine how much must come from other sources, i.e. the money that you may have to seek from other people. Figure out how much you will need to ask for, and when.

Finally, construct a budget for your life after divorce, when the dust has settled and you've received your share of the family assets and support, if any. How much will be available for paying back the money that's been lent to you? How fast will you be able to pay that money back? Make sure you're being reasonable, and fight the urge to be overly optimistic. Remember, when asking for loans from loved ones or friends, it's important to be upfront and honest about when you expect to be able to repay the money, and how long the repayments are likely to take. Err on the side of pessimism. Remember the business adage "promise less and deliver more." This is a very good rule to live by in sensitive financial dealings among friends and family.

One last note: Let's say that your divorce and your financial settlement go pretty much as you planned, and you come to the light at the end of the tunnel when you can finally begin paying back the money that your friends or family have lent to you. Unless you have funds in hand to pay back the entire sum without risking your future ability to pay your bills, don't fork over all your cash in one fell swoop, no matter how much you might want to in order to alleviate your loved ones' fears about getting their money back and assuage your guilt about having taken it. It's better to start a regimen of monthly payments, and stick to it, than to hand over a wad of money only to have to turn around later and ask for some or all of it back. Remind yourself that as long as you adhere to your promise to pay X dollars every X months, you will maintain the trust and respect of those who helped you. Don't do anything to undermine that, even if for the best intentions.

Be Realistic In Your Expectations

It's surprising how warped a person's view can be when contemplating the process of divorce. One spouse may have fallen in love with someone new and be so high on the new surge of happiness that he or she blindly believes that everything will just fall into place, their spouse will be as happy as they are to end their marriage, and all will be lovely soon. Another spouse might think her husband is literally out of his mind so she expects to face outrageous battles about anything and everything that must be decided during the divorce, so she gears up to push back and fight with all her might over every issue that comes up.

Try to be objective, to the extent possible, in anticipating what is likely to happen as you proceed through your divorce. Face honestly the question of whether you and your partner both really want a divorce. Will you be working for the same ultimate goal, albeit with different hoped-for outcomes, or are you at loggerheads over the simple matter of divorcing in the first place? Will your husband be out to punish you every step of the way, or will he be more likely to wave away most areas of conflict with a "let's just get this done and not get bogged down" attitude? Is there likely to be interference from other family members? Do you think your husband will lie, cheat, and steal as much as he can, or will he be honest and honorable when it comes to divulging financial information and dividing up assets? Is violence possible? Is there a chance your husband will move far away, and want to take the children with him?

Think through what is likely to transpire, as best you can, and sit down with both your lawyer and your financial advisor and paint a picture of who they will be dealing with when they are representing you. They will be better prepared to do their best for you, and they will be better equipped to offer relevant up-front advice about protecting your assets, your children, and your sanity as you move through this painful process.

Lastly, don't nickel and dime your lawyer. You probably don't try to negotiate the cost of your highlights with your hairdresser. Why would it be ok to haggle with the person who is fighting for your rights and for your future? If you trust the person you've hired and they have a reputation for honesty, then they are most likely not over billing you and in fact, they probably spend considerable time on your file that is not reflected on your bill. The last thing you want is for your case to become the case that everyone in the office hates. It's hard for a lawyer to prioritize a client who either constantly complains about the bill or refuses to pay or honor her payment plan.

Research:
1. Family law attorney Carla Schiff Donnelly says, "There is no substitute for word of mouth when it comes to hiring an attorney. Financial advisors, therapists, attorneys practicing in other areas and CPAs usually know good divorce attorneys, as do people who

have been divorced in the last couple of years." Her article, "Don't Get Stuck With The Wrong Lawyer: 6 Steps To Avoid the Most Common Divorce Mistake," was published in the *Huffington Post.* http://www.huffingtonpost.com/carla-schiff-donnelly-/divorce-attorney_b_4003476.html

2. District judge The Honorable Anne Kass advises, find a good divorce lawyer, not a fighter, in "How to Find a Good Divorce Attorney vs a Fighter Attorney - Some tips from a judge on finding the right divorce lawyer." http://www.alllaw.com/articles/family/divorce/article38.asp

3. Lawyers.com has a large listing of divorce lawyers or law firms by state. http://www.lawyers.com/divorce/find-law-firms-by-location/?gclid=Cj0KEQjw58ytBRDMg-HVn4LuqasBEiQAhPkh uo9uHuQ_STkoESp30G0y4SwBXSmYcNeyc3iy5EZoNsoaAm-s8P8HAQ&ef_id=VaWgRgAAAIssPDoC:20150726001637:s

4. FindLaw.com also has a state-by-state listing of attorneys, at http://lawyers.findlaw.com/lawyer/practice/divorce

5. "Researching Attorney Discipline." http://hirealawyer.findlaw.com/choosing-the-right-lawyer/researching-attorney-discipline.html

6. For a discussion of how to find the divorce lawyer who's right for you, and what questions you should ask when interviewing lawyers, see "Family Law: Selecting a Good Lawyer." http://family-law.lawyers.com/family-law-selecting-a-good-lawyer.html

7. Bankrate.com's information-packed article, "Finding a financial planner," features a helpful list of tips for selecting a financial advisor, along with links to several resources to help you in your search. http://www.bankrate.com/finance/financial-literacy/finding-a-financial-planner-1.aspx

8. You can verify an individual's CFP certification and background on the CFP Board's website, at http://www.cfp.net/utility/verify-an-individual-s-cfp-certification-and-background

9. Belinda Rachman discusses the pros and cons of using a divorce lawyer versus a mediator, in "Which is Right for You, Mediation or a Divorce Lawyer?" http://divorcesupport.about.com/od/divorceattorneys/f/Med_Lawyer.htm

10. The American Academy of Matrimonial Lawyers has published a comprehensive discussion and guide to lawyer's fees you should expect and various arrangements for payment that might be possible. See http://www.aaml.org/library/publications/415/divorce-manual-client-handbook/13-attorneys-fees-and-costs

Chapter 15
Monetary Objectives

There's so much planning to do that it may feel like it takes all the energy you can muster to figure out how you'll pay your bills and daily expenses, plus your legal and advisor fees as you work through your divorce. In this context, the actual divorce settlement that looms ahead of you might start to take on the cast of a shining place you will reach when it's all over, where all will be saved.

Don't fall into that trap. First, you cannot assume anything now about what you will be awarded in the way of asset division and alimony when all is said and done. And even if you do receive everything you hoped for, you must face the fact that even if it's more than you're living on now, it may not be enough to keep you living in quite the lifestyle that you would like. First of all, you may have debts to repay if family or friends have loaned you money during the divorce. There may be some extra expenses in your new single life for repairs and maintenance that your husband used to take care of. And, quite simply, supporting a household of your own with one income, supplemented perhaps by alimony and/or child support, is simply not as cost efficient as supporting a home with two incomes and two adults who can perform the work to keep up the place and make repairs when needed.

Then there's always the unknown hanging over your head: Will your husband actually pay what he's been ordered to do? If he does, will he pay on time? Will you end up having to incur additional legal expenses for injunctive relief or wage garnishment or other methods of enforcing your support award? From a financial aspect, life most likely is going to be leaner than it was before.

If you were the major breadwinner throughout your marriage and it's likely that you will be paying alimony to your husband rather than the other way around, you can't know until the award is made exactly how much that will be, nor for how long. Brace yourself for the additional expense you are going to be carrying on top of the loss of assets and cash that will happen when the estate is divided.

So concentrate now on what you can fairly expect the division of assets to be. How do you determine what's fair? How much input do you really have into what should be divided and how? Your attorney's advice is invaluable in examining the possibilities and making decisions.

I Can't Say This Enough: Listen To Your Lawyer

I have to say that it can be quite frustrating, from an attorney's point of view, at this stage of the game in the divorce. Some clients are so angry at their spouses that they want to punish and punish and punish and they simply cannot see how it's fair if their husband gets anything close to what they themselves will take away. It can take real work to talk a wife down who's been wronged, especially if there's been infidelity or abuse. But the cold, hard, and logical fact is that rightful ownership of assets, possessions, and money is based on legal rights and equitable principles, not on who's the biggest jerk around. When you're reeling with hurt feelings and rage, it can simply be impossible to feel that it's fair that your husband should get half of everything.

But if that's how it sorts out under the law, that's how it sorts out. You must take a deep breath and accept it. You are not the mother imbued with the authority to mete out punishment for your very bad child. You are the partner to a contract which has been breached and is now being terminated, and you must divide the assets fairly according to who owns what and who has legal rights and claims against the other. It's just the way it is, so set your mind and get through it as rationally as you can. If you need to vent, try to direct your anger into your therapy sessions, an evening over wine with a girlfriend, journaling, or sessions with your spiritual advisor. Money will not cure what you're feeling.

On the other hand, what if you're drowning in guilt because *you* decided to bring the marriage to an end? This can be especially difficult if you've found someone else, you've had an affair, and now you are quite deliriously happy to be with your new love. Your instinct may be to "just let my husband have everything" because you feel you owe your soon-to-be-ex as much consolation as you can give.

Money is not the way to do that. Yes, you can be generous with the division of memorabilia if you think that will comfort your husband in some way, you can (and should) be careful to avoid any negative statements about your ex in front of your children, and you should do your best to be as efficient as possible in producing the paperwork, making decisions, and generally moving the painful process along so it can be over as soon as possible.

But don't give away your money. It's yours every bit as much as it is his, and you'd be a fool to put yourself in sackcloth and ashes, financially speaking, to "prove" how bad you feel about what you've done. You may have behaved badly or hurtfully, but you have not lost your legal rights to what's rightfully yours. Keep a level head. Protect your own financial future, and that of your children. Take what's fairly yours, and no apologies or guilt over it. Your husband is (or should be) a big boy and can take care of himself just as well as you can take care of yourself. Give him credit for being able to get back on his feet and go on, with his fair share of the estate and without *your* share in his pocket too.

So whether you want more than is fair or less, this juncture in the process is where it may be hardest to listen to your attorney's advice, because your instincts are pushing you in a different direction than your attorney is telling you to go. Let that be a sign to you that this is precisely the point where you should pay close attention to what your lawyer is saying to you, and follow his or her direction. Believe me, divorce lawyers have seen it all and they know darn well what's likely to happen as the process moves along. Use their expertise. Believe in the value of their experience in handling many divorces before yours. Let them help you. That's what you're paying them for. Your attorney has your best interests at heart, and the minds and means to bring you the best outcome possible, so please, follow his or her advice. In five years, you'll look back and you will thank yourself.

Once You See Where You're Going, Plan Your Future

Once you've developed a fairly clear picture of what you're going to walk away with, when all is said and done, do some real planning now. In your planning, include all the scenarios that may come to pass, from good to imperfect to awful.

Now it's time to run the numbers, several times over. You might want to do this on different days in order to clear your head of the thoughts you're having regarding any given outcome scenario.

First let's look at how things will shape up if indeed everything you own is split 50-50 and you're awarded alimony in the amount that you feel is fair. Put those numbers down on a piece of paper and start working out a budget from there. What will you be able to afford in the way of housing, a car, education for the children, clothing, and so on?

Remember as you fill in the items under the expenses section, that you will need to adjust some expenses upward or downward from your past life, based on your current circumstances. Food costs will be lower with one less adult in the picture, as will gas, auto maintenance, clothing, medical expenses, and miscellaneous items such as haircuts and gym memberships. Other costs may be higher; new or extra counseling sessions for the children, childcare costs to cover situations where your husband used to watch the kids, household repairs your husband used to do himself, a maid service because you no longer have the time to take care of cleaning.

Now think ahead to the day when alimony will stop. Do you expect to receive alimony for a year, several years, or for life? What will you do when it ends? You must plan for the day, eventually, when your husband will no longer be supplementing your income. It can be hard to face or plan for that time, because it's a negative thought. Many women develop a blind spot about this eventual outcome; they reason, consciously or subconsciously, that by the time that day comes, they will have progressed in their career or grown their business or found another man and their own income will have grown so much that the drop in alimony payments won't matter. It's very hard not to think that way, because of course that is positive thinking and it's better to be an optimist than a pessimist, right?

Wrong. In most matters, it's of course better to practice positive thinking, but not when it comes to financial planning. Too much optimism can sink you. You must *plan* only on the known and *prepare* always for the unknown.

So what will happen if you don't receive the raises you hoped you would, or your business doesn't expand as you imagined, or you don't meet and marry (or join households with) someone new? You must plan for these possibilities in the unknown that is your future after alimony. This means living in a home that costs a little less than your cash flow today can actually handle, going out less often than your bank account says you can afford to do, taking more modest vacations than you might want to, limiting the activities and other discretionary expenses that you allow for your children. I know it's very difficult to do, because most newly divorced women *don't* do it. And I do understand why. It's been a long struggle. You want to do everything you can to make life go back to normal, for yourself and for your kids. You're determined to keep a positive attitude and enjoy life.

That's all well and good, but you must always keep in mind that you're traveling along a steady and relentless drive toward a steep cliff. Perhaps you have thousands of miles to go because you've been awarded alimony for many years – but the cliff you're heading toward is there nevertheless. If you don't want to fall straight off of it when the time comes, you need to alter your course bit by bit as you travel. If down the road you *do* get a big raise, or grow your company's profits, or meet a wealthy and wonderful man who wants to marry you, so much the better. But if you do not, you will know that you've done everything you can to keep from reaching that precipice and going over. You may not live in as nice a home as you would like or wear the designer shoes you love or be able to say yes to everything your children want, but you'll be providing yourself and your kids much more security in life, and believe me, you'll sleep better at night.

Planning For The Worst What If

What if your husband doesn't pay? Roughly 34% of fathers in the United States are under an order to pay child support to their children right now. According to *Time Magazine*, in 2011, only 61% of child support payments were made by men to the mothers of their children. There are many reasons why this may happen; the father simply doesn't have the financial means to pay; or he's choosing to make in-kind contributions rather than cash, even though that choice is not sanctioned by the court; or his wife has refused to allow visitation and the two former spouses are engaged in another battle royale, with their children the unfortunate pawns, and victims, of the war; or the dad is, quite simply, a deadbeat.

Regardless of whether you believe your husband is going to actually deliver the support payments that have been ordered, or not, or pay them in a timely fashion or only after repeated delays, you must plan for the "what if" scenario that will unfold if he does not pay you and pay you on time. How will you live and pay the bills then? Do you have savings? A line of credit? Even credit cards with unused credit available? Think about your back-up system and how you can make it more solid. It's best to do this thinking before you make decisions about where to live and where to send your children to school and how to spend your discretionary funds, if possible. If you avoid locking yourself into a lifestyle that uses up every penny that comes into your bank account every month, you can set a little bit of money aside each month and create a growing cushion against disaster should the support payments dry up.

What If You Know You Deserve More?

If you suspect that your husband might have hidden some assets, tell your lawyer about it as soon as you have any knowledge or even an inkling that this may be true. It's not too late even if the divorce decree has been finalized, because that decree was made based upon information available to you and the court at the time that it was issued. If new information has come to light since then, you have the right to seek an amendment of your decree and to obtain your fair share of whatever money or property might have been hidden away during the divorce proceedings. While the burden will be upon you to prove that those assets exist and what they're worth, remember that you have the power of the discovery process on your side. If you and your lawyer can show cause, the court can issue an order to your husband to produce documents and other information that may help identify the whereabouts and value of assets he's hiding. Don't wait to take action. The longer you delay, the colder the paper trail and the harder it may be to prove your case.

The Bigger Picture

When you begin the process of divorce, you immediately become the master of your own fate. Think of yourself throughout the ordeal as the Independent You, not the Wronged Wife. Look your financial future in the eye. Many women who divorce suffer tremendous financial losses, but few prepare for that fact. You may hate it, but you cannot make it go away. Face the fact that your income, your style of living, and your prospects for retirement are likely going to drop significantly. Accept the challenge to minimize the damage and the downfall as much as you possibly can, and put all of your efforts into planning and preparing. Your life post-divorce will be the better for it.

Research:

1. *Forbes* contributor Jeff Landers points out the most common financial pitfalls for women going through divorce, in "Three Types of Financial Mistakes Divorcing Women Make (And How to Avoid Them)."
http://www.forbes.com/sites/jefflanders/2012/11/27/three-types-of-financial-mistakes-divorcing-women-make-and-how-to-avoid-them/

2. Landers also makes some extremely good points about being prepared and being organized, in "Why Women Who Are Organized Often Do Better in Divorce." This really gets at the heart of this book – if you're smart, organized, prepared, and armed with knowledge and confidence, you'll come out on top (or at least not on the bottom) whether you're single, happily married, or going through the collapse of your marriage.
http://www.forbes.com/sites/jefflanders/2012/03/27/why-women-who-are-organized-often-do-better-in-divorce/

3. Ginita Wall, CPA, CFP, details "The Twelve Financial Pitfalls of Divorce," at http://www.wife.org/12-financial-pitfalls-of-divorce.htm. Her most priceless piece of advice: "During divorce, prepare yourself mentally for the worst that can happen. How will you cope if your children get sick? If you have to move in with your parents? If the divorce lasts for years and you lose all of your money? If your ex remarries within two weeks, moves to Tahiti, and/or refuses to pay any support? Plan for the worst so what actually happens will seem easy by comparison. Don't panic and let your fears rule your life. Face them, and take control."

4. Statistics on dads who do not pay child support are eye-opening, not only for the numbers of men who don't pay, but because of the reasons why. Read through this list of "why's" on Brandon Gaille's website to see how the actions of the mother, post-divorce, can influence her chances of receiving the payments

she's been awarded:

a. Over 90% of the fathers who are ordered to pay child support do so when they receive joint custody of their children.

b. Only 44.5% of fathers who receive no visitation rights choose to pay court ordered child support.

c. 25% of single mothers with full custodial support don't receive any child support because the father cannot afford to pay it.

d. 20% of single mothers have made agreements with fathers outside of the court system to pay for child needs.

e. Among single mothers, 11% do not have any child support orders whatsoever.

f. Deadbeat dads account for 7% of the cases of child support not being paid. That translates into 1 out of every 14 families. "23 Important Deadbeat Dads Statistics," http://brandongaille.com/23-deadbeat-dads-statistics/

5. In "How Deadbeat are Deadbeat Dads, Really?," *Time* writer Belinda Luscombe discusses studies and theories that explain why some dads don't give the cash payments to their children that they've been court ordered to make. http://time.com/3921605/deadbeat-dads/

Chapter 16

Self-Sufficiently Ever After

When a divorce is finalized, it's time to look forward, not back. You've arrived on the other side. No matter what you've been through or how painful the process has been, you can be thankful that it's over now. Here you are. This is what it is. How are you going to make the best of it?

Life may not be simple or smooth at this stage, but one big improvement has taken place; you're done with the arguing and negotiating and decision making and signing of papers. The psychological burden of being in the middle of the struggle has lifted - and now you have at least a little extra time for yourself. This is the time for honest self-reflection.

Take some time to think about what you learned – not just through the divorce but through the entire marriage. Can you see now that you were blind to some red flags about your spouse that are very obvious to you in hindsight? Did you excuse too many inexcusable behaviors? Did you lay low and hope for the best when, in retrospect, you now realize you should have spoken up or taken action?

And what about your own shortcomings? Can you be honest about your share of the blame for the relationship failing? Did you make your husband try to guess what you were thinking or what you wanted? Did you tend to ignore your husband and his needs? Did you play a little fast and loose with the disposable cash in the household? Did you tend to make unilateral decisions when you wanted to make sure you got what you wanted?

It's all a learning experience, whether you were blameless or contributed to the problems, and whether the outcome was entirely foreseeable or not. Don't chalk up the whole relationship as a big mistake. It wasn't. There were legitimate reasons that you fell in love and decided to get married in the first place – but maybe they were blown out of proportion or you gave too much weight to certain factors

140

and not enough to others in your assessment of your husband as the ideal mate. You started out with good intentions, and most likely so did he. Try to puzzle out where the missteps happened and when the snowball effect started to take over. Make a conscious effort to be utterly honest with yourself and vow to use the awareness you've gained both of others and of yourself to guide you in the next relationship you enter into.

Wisdom

What would you have done differently in your marriage, if you'd known then what you know now? Perhaps you've learned that when you rely on a messy history to interpret current actions or statements, you can often go off the mark in understanding your mate. Or you've come to understand that if you don't share at least a common core of interests with a potential spouse (other than sex), then your chance of maintaining connection and harmony through shared experiences may be compromised over time. Or you've learned that it doesn't work to nurse your anger toward your spouse and expect him to figure out what the problem is without telling him directly.

The more you can dig out nuggets of understanding and points of insight from what has happened, the better you will be able to navigate a future relationship successfully. And, frankly, the better you will be able to forgive and forget – both the mistakes and the wrongdoings of your spouse and those you committed yourself. Invest the time in thinking through what happened and what you can learn from it.

Lessons Learned

Now that you're free of the past, or at least free of the work of extricating yourself from the past, what will you take with you going forward? What new operating principles will you put in place if or when you marry again? Will you be more careful to express your appreciation for kindness and fair treatment? Will you devote a little more conscious attention to the way you spend your time together than you did before? Will you vow to set aside a night once a month to review your bank and credit card statements together and compare your income and expenditures to what you planned in your budget? Allow your insights and your new rules for living and loving to guide you on a better path next time around.

Putting Your Financial House In Order Once Again

It's time to put your own finances in order, now that the negotiations are over, you've received your share of the estate, and you know what you'll be receiving from your ex in the way of alimony and/or child support. You've got concrete numbers to work with now, so pull out those old "What If" planning sheets you worked on in Chapter 15, and start a new sheet for "What Now."

First, get a fresh credit report

Obtain your current credit histories from all three reporting agencies. Be prepared, after the upheaval you've just been through, to find incorrect information on your record – a little or a lot. Make sure your address is correct. If you're no longer on a credit card account that was a joint account before, make sure you notify the credit agency that you are no longer a user of or responsible for that account. If debts or loans have been paid off but are not reflected in your record, clear that up. It's easy to correct misinformation on your credit reports. Search each site and you will find links for reporting what's wrong and supplying the correct information.

Do keep notes of every update and correction you submitted to the credit bureaus, and mark your calendar to check back again with them to see that the necessary corrections have been made. You want to be absolutely certain to keep a clean and up-to-date credit file from this point forward.

Of course, there may be black marks on your credit report that are up-to-date and that you therefore cannot remove from your record. Take these seriously and work to clear them away as quickly as you can. It's not as though you'll be arrested by the "credit police" for having negative information on your report, but you will suffer for it when you apply for a credit card, a loan, a mortgage, or possibly even a lease on an apartment. Set a goal to clear up the bad stuff as quickly as you can; bring late payments up to date, pay down balances that are too high, and settle disputes if there are any noted on your record.

If you need assistance with debt and credit problems, get help

If there are more problems with your credit history than you can handle, then get help. There are several reputable debt counseling services out there. They can assist you with information on a variety of ways to tackle your problems, reduce your debt, and clear up your record. For example, you might be able to lower the interest rates on some of your credit cards by simply making phone calls to your credit card companies, explaining that you're having a hardship, and requesting a lower rate. There may be a mortgage assistance program you qualify for. You might be able to consolidate several debts into one loan at a lower rate with a longer repayment period. A good debt counseling service also will give you guidance on how to pare down your budget, manage expenses, and create a long-term debt reduction game plan that you can live with.

When looking for a debt assistance service to help you, be very careful. Unfortunately, if you're in a money bind, you're automatically part of a target market encircled by plenty of sharks who are ready, willing, and able to feed off of your desperation. So screen the service you will use. You can inquire about debt counseling services at universities, military bases, credit unions, housing authorities, branches of the U.S. Cooperative Extension Service, your financial institution, your local consumer protection agency, and friends and family.

Be aware that "non-profit" status doesn't guarantee that services are free, affordable, or even legitimate. The Federal Trade Commission advises that a reputable credit counseling agency should send you free information about itself and the services it provides without requiring you to provide any details about your situation.

For any counseling agency you find that seems promising, check it out with your state Attorney General and local consumer protection agency to see if any complaints have been lodged against it. Then when you think you've found the agency that can help you, go through this set of questions to screen them:

- **What services do you offer?** Look for an organization that offers a range of services, including budget counseling and savings and debt management classes. Stay away from organizations that insist you enter into their debt management plan (DMP). It might be a good choice for you, but it should not be your only choice.

- **Do you offer free information?** The answer should be yes.
- **In addition to helping me solve my problem today, will you help me work out a plan for my future financial health?** Again, they should be prepared to do this for you.
- **What are your fees?** Are there set-up and/or monthly fees? Get a specific price quote in writing.
- **What if I can't afford to pay your fees?** If the answer is that they cannot help you, then don't fork out any money. Look for another agency to work with.
- **Where is your written agreement?** Insist on having everything in writing, signed by both parties, and make sure your agreement includes the assurance that all of your information, including your address, phone number, and financial information, will be kept strictly confidential.
- **Are you licensed to offer your services in my state?** Ask for proof.
- **What are your counselors' qualifications?**
- **Are your employees paid incentive fees if I sign up for certain services or pay a fee?** Don't use their services if they are.

Develop a Good Reputation At Your Bank

Whether you have a stellar credit record or a shabby one, develop a relationship with your bank. Make yourself known to one of the managers. Ask for information or advice in person when it's needed rather than by calling the bank's 800 number. And keep your account or accounts in good order. Monitor your activities and balances online and make sure you don't have overdraws or late fees. One day you may need to apply for a loan or even just a new credit card. If you are known to your banker and you've been conscientious about keeping on top of your banking activities, you will have a leg up when you go through the application process.

Live Within Your Means

Now that you've worked to clean up your credit records and you've come up with a plan for managing debt and ultimately removing any bad marks from your records with the credit bureaus, review your budget once again. You may need to tweak it – and interestingly, you might find that it's easier to do so once you've started to feel that you're getting your life back in order.

Work on that budget once again to fit with your life as it is now, not what you hope it will be soon, and stick with it. Keep reminding yourself that maintaining the ability to pay your bills on time and reduce your debts brings far more enjoyment than fancy homes, cars, or clothing. You know this to be true, but the more you live it, the more you will *feel* it to be true too.

You're Not Alone

Even though the divorce process is over, your relationships with your attorney and financial advisor are not. These are the people you should turn to as matters come up that require their counsel or assistance. They know you best, they know your history, and they have a good handle on your goals and capabilities. The attorney and financial advisor you know may help you directly, or they may direct you to another professional better equipped to handle the question or problem at hand, but they are the best place to start.

Make it a habit to get expert advice when you need it, and the earlier the better. If you seek guidance before important decisions are made or as soon as problems rear their heads, you will minimize mistakes and enhance your chances for positive outcomes. An investment in expert advice is well worth the cost.

CHECKLIST OF IDEAS AND RESOURCES TO GET THROUGH YOUR DIVORCE

1. Find a hobby. Sometimes we have to act our way into feeling better, and finding an activity that you find rewarding or that allows you to be creative is a great way to move on.
2. Search online. There are hundreds of websites, blogs and forums dedicated to helping women get through a divorce.
3. Find a therapist. Look for a woman you can relate to and whom you feel comfortable with sharing your feelings without judgment.
4. Stay within your budget. You're already feeling the pangs of the divorce; don't add financial insecurity into the mix.
5. Start a journal. It's a private place where you can be completely honest and not worry about judgments, because the contents is for your eyes only.
6. Meditation. It does not have to be the sitting cross-legged variety of meditation. Give yourself 20 minutes per day to be alone with your thoughts, to honor your feelings and to discover yourself again in an authentic way. "Within you there is a stillness and a sanctuary to which you can retreat at anytime and be yourself." Hermann Hesse
7. Try to have fun. Try new things. Start a book club, a monthly meeting with your girlfriends to try a new restaurant each time, or even start dating again. There is lots of advice out there on how to jump back into the dating pool. Take advantage of the information that is out there and learn from the experiences of others. You may be getting the chance to reinvent yourself.
8. Don't be afraid. Eleanor Roosevelt suggested that we "do one thing every day that scares you." Try it and you may find yourself succeeding at things you didn't even imagine were possible.

Research:

1. *Scary Mommy* lists ten very practical things you must do or need to have when you go through a divorce and become a single parent. http://www.scarymommy.com/articles/how-to-survive-as-a-newly-single-parent?section=single-parenting&u=QMyAvUdl mJ

2. In "Seven Ways to Thrive After Divorce," Mark Banschick M.D. offers tips on getting over it and getting on after a divorce, with advice that's more practical and less clichéd than many articles you'll find on this topic. https://www.psychologytoday.com/blog/the-intelligent-divorce/201309/seven-ways-thrive-after-divorce

3. Adult education classes can be a great way to beef up your skills or knowledge in areas that you might have left to your husband prior to your divorce, and they can be a comfortable and safe way to do a little socializing too. Check out your local community center, city resources, and community colleges in your area for courses on everything from household bookkeeping to financial planning to simple home repairs.

4. For a detailed article from the Federal Trade Commission on how to choose a credit counselor and the scams and red flags to look out for in the process of finding one, see "Choosing A Credit Counselor." https://www.consumer.ftc.gov/articles/0153-choosing-credit-counselor

GLOSSARY OF LEGAL TERMS

Action: Another word for lawsuit.

Affidavit: A written statement taken under oath that is signed in the presence of a notary public.

Agreement: Generally, a written resolution of the outstanding issues that is signed by the parties and is also some times referred to as a Stipulation.

Alimony: A sum that is paid by one party to the other on a monthly basis for a specific timeframe or in a lump sum.

Alimony pendente lite: Alimony that is paid after the divorce petition has been filed and while the divorce is in progress, prior to the final order.

Allegations: Written or oral statements contained in a pleading or motion that set forth what the party is going to prove.

Annulment: Grounds for annulment vary from state to state. It is the legal ending of an invalid marriage such that the parties are found to have never been married but all children born to the parties remain legitimate.

Answer: The second pleading in a divorce, separation, or annulment, which is served in response to the petition for divorce and which admits or denies the petition's allegations and may also make claims against the other party. Sometimes called a Response.

Appeal: The process during which a higher court reviews the proceedings from a lower court proceeding and determines if there was reversible error or it affirms the lower court's order.

Appearance: The attorney of record's formal method of advising the court and all interested parties that she or he represents either the petitioner or the respondent. Appearance also can refer to a party's physical presence in court.

Child support: Financial support for a child (not taxable to the recipient or deductible to the payor spouse).

Contempt of court: The willful and intentional failure to comply with a court order, judgment, or decree by a party to the action, which may be punishable in a variety of ways, including but not limited to sanctions and incarceration.

Contested case: Any case where there are issues that must be decided by the court because the parties are not in agreement.

Court order: A written document issued by a court that is only effective when signed by a judge.

Cross-examination: The questioning of a witness by the opposing party during a trial or at a deposition, to test the truth of that testimony or to develop it. During cross-examination, the party asking the questions can lead the witness toward yes or no answers – this is not allowed on direct examination.

Custody: The legal right and responsibility awarded by a court for the care, possession, and rearing of a child. Distinctions are sometimes made between legal custody, which relates to decision making responsibility, and physical custody, which relates to residence or physical access. In some jurisdictions, the concept of custody has been written out of the laws so that only decision making authority is resolved and the amount of time one party will spend with the children versus the other party.

Default: When one party fails to respond or appear within the required timeframe, the clerk either on their own or by motion of the other party enters an order that states that that party failed to respond and the other party may proceed without further involvement by the defaulting party.

Defendant/Respondent: The person (husband or wife) who is sued for divorce.

Direct examination: The initial questioning in court or in deposition of a witness by the lawyer who called him or her to the stand or noticed him or her for deposition. During direct examination the questioner may not lead the witness toward the response. Generally, the question should not result in a yes or a no answer.

Disclosure/discovery/production of documents: The part of the case that all parties hate because they have to gather volumes of documents, typically of a financial nature. It is during the discovery process that a lawyer assesses the case to determine the nature, scope, and credibility of the opposing party's claim and his or her financial status.

Dissolution: The act of terminating a marriage, often referred to as the Initial Dissolution of Marriage proceedings.

Emancipation: The point when a child is legally considered an adult and in most states when the duty to support may terminate.

Equitable Distribution: A legal concept that creates a scheme for dividing the parties' assets and liabilities. Equitable does not mean Equal, in some cases. Several factors are considered such as when an asset/debt was acquired, whether the asset/debt has non marital characteristics, etc.

Evidence: Testimony, documents and other demonstrative material that are offered in court to prove or disprove allegations.

Ex parte: A Latin term that refers to a communication with the court that is made without the other party being present or notified. Most ex parte communications are prohibited.

Grounds: The reasons argued or included in a motion or pleading to support granting the relief being asked for by either side.

Guardian ad litem (GAL): A lawyer or mental health professional that is appointed by the court on behalf of the minor children. The GAL is not the lawyer for the children, in that he or she does not advocate a position for the children and the GAL is not the judge.

Hearing: Any proceeding before a court on an issue that is disputed between the parties. Some hearings require evidence and some hearings require only legal argument.

Hold-harmless: A party may assume responsibility for a debt and he or she promises to shield the other spouse from any liability (responsibility) as it pertains to that debt.

Indemnification: The promise to reimburse another person in case of an anticipated loss or involvement in a lawsuit.

Injunction: A court order forbidding someone from acting in a certain way that is likely to cause injury to a person or property loss to another party; the same as a restraining order.

Interrogatories: A series of written questions served on the opposing party to discover certain facts regarding the disputed issues in a matrimonial proceeding. The answer to interrogatories must be under oath and served within a prescribed time.

Joint Custody: The shared right and responsibility of both parents awarded by the court for possession, care, and rearing of the children. The concept of "custody" has fallen out of favor.

Joint property: Property held in the name of more than one person.

Jurisdiction: The authority of the court to rule on issues relating to the parties, their children, or their property.

Legal separation: A court judgment or written agreement directing or authorizing spouses to live separate and apart. A decree of separation does not dissolve the marriage or allow the parties to remarry, but may resolve all financial claims.

Maintenance: Spousal support. See also alimony.

Marital property: Accumulated income and property acquired by spouses, subject to certain exclusions in some states.

Marital settlement agreement: The parties' settlement is reduced to a written document or orally placed on the record in open court. This agreement also may be called a property settlement agreement or separation agreement. It should be signed by both parties and if a transfer of real estate is involved, it should contain two witnesses and be notarized.

Mediation: A process by which a neutral third party facilitates negotiations between the parties. The mediator generally has no decision-making authority and the process is privileged and confidential.

Motion: A written application to the court for some particular relief, such as temporary support, temporary parenting plan, temporary attorney fees and costs, injunction, exclusive use and possession, or for expert's fees, etc.

Motion to modify: A party's formal written request to the court to change a prior order regarding custody, child support, alimony, or any other order that the court may change by law. A motion may only be used if it is a temporary order; otherwise, modifications must be by supplemental petition.

Motion to vacate the premises: Upon a showing of good cause by one party, the court orders the other spouse to leave the marital residence.

No fault divorce: When divorce is granted without a party having to prove the other party's marital misconduct. "Fault" is marital misconduct that may be considered for some issues in some states.

Notice of hearing: A document that is served on the opposing lawyer or spouse listing the date and place of a hearing and the motion or motions that will be heard by the court and the length of time reserved for the hearing.

Order: The court's ruling on a motion requiring the parties to do certain things or setting forth their rights and responsibilities. An order is reduced to writing, signed by the judge, and filed with the court.

Party: (plural: parties) Typically refers to the Wife and Husband in a divorce but can also refer to anyone involved in the action whose interests may be affected, such as the Guardian ad Litem.

Petition: Referred to in civil court as the "complaint," it is the first pleading in an action for divorce, separate maintenance, or annulment, setting forth the allegations on which the requested relief is based.

Petitioner (plaintiff): The party who files the petition for divorce or any other petition.

Pleading: Formal written application to the court for relief and the written response to it. Pleadings include petitions, answers, counter-claims and replies.

Privilege: The right of a person to make statements to his or her spouse or lawyer, member of the clergy, psychiatrist, doctor, or certified social worker that are not later admissible in evidence.

Pro se: A party or litigant who is representing himself or herself and is not represented by a lawyer.

Relief: Whatever a party to a divorce proceeding asks the court to do: dissolve the marriage, award support, enforce a prior court order or decree, divide property, enjoin certain behavior, dismiss the complaint of the other party, and so on.

Reply: The pleading filed in answer to allegations of a counterclaim or to affirmative defenses.

Report of referee/general magistrate: The written document prepared by a referee or court-appointed officer after a hearing and submitted to the parties (husband and wife) and the judge; it is not law and not final or an order of the court, but it is recommended to become an order of the court. The court must decide whether to approve and ratify the recommendations or not.

Respondent (defendant): The one who answers or defends the divorce proceeding brought by another.

Request for production of documents: Part of the discovery process, this is a_series of written requests served on the other party seeking the production of documents, such as financial records. Responses must be provided within a fixed time.

Rules of evidence: The rules that govern the presentation and admissibility of oral and documentary evidence at court hearings or depositions.

Separate Property: Property that is not part of the marital estate because it belongs solely to one spouse. It is not "marital property."

Set off: A debt or financial obligation of one spouse that is deducted from the debt or financial gain or obligation of the other spouse.

Settlement: The agreed resolution of disputed issues.

Show cause: Written application to the court for some type of relief, which is made on such notice to the other party as the court directs.

Stipulation: An agreement between the parties or their counsel.

Subpoena: A document served on a party or witness requiring appearance in court or deposition. Failure to comply with the subpoena could result in punishment by the court. A subpoena duces tecum is a subpoena requesting that the party bring documents to the deposition or hearing that are presumably relevant to the proceeding.

Summons: A written notification that legal action has commenced, requiring a response within a specified time period.

Temporary or pendente lite motions: Applications to the court for interim relief pending the final decree of divorce, separation, or annulment. Typical temporary motions include motions for temporary maintenance, child support, attorney's fees, costs, expert fees, custody, visitation, enforcement, or modification of prior temporary orders, or requests for exclusive possession. The court enters a pendente lite order after determining a motion.

Temporary restraining order (TRO): An order of the court prohibiting a party from doing something such as threatening, harassing, stalking or beating the other spouse or the children, selling personal property, withdrawing money from accounts, denying access to a motor vehicle, etc.

Testimony: Statements under oath by a witness in court or during a deposition.

Transcript: A record of the testimony taken by a court reporter during a deposition or court proceeding that includes references to all exhibits marked and/or entered as evidence.

Trial: The final step in a litigation, it is a formal court proceeding where the party has to present their case with testimony and exhibits and the judge must decide on all contested issues.

Uncontested Divorce: A perfunctory divorce proceeding that results in the final order dissolving the parties' marriage that can be completed if the parties enter into a settlement agreement.

STEP-BY-STEP GUIDE TO INSURE THAT YOU PROTECT YOUR LEGAL RIGHTS, YOUR ASSETS, YOUR CHILDREN, AND YOUR PHYSICAL AND MENTAL HEALTH

The difference between you in charge and you lost and blindsided are:
1. Organization
2. Knowledge
3. Determination

Essentially, if you assume responsibility for what's going on financially and legally in your life, and you maintain control over your physical and mental well-being and that of your children – whether you're single, happily married, or in the throes of divorce – you will reap the best possible outcomes throughout your life.

So, here are the steps to take to insure that you do just that:

Paperwork

If you're a filing freak and know where every form, contract, statement, and set of instructions is, more power to you. And we hope you're not too lonely, because most people do not live in your world. Most are not the best when it comes to organizing and maintaining paperwork, especially at home. If filing and paperwork are not your forte, that's OK – but that's not an excuse for letting everything fall into a disorganized mess. You must be on top of the paperwork that houses records, proves ownership, specifies rights, and records important histories such as medical records.

Gather and keep all files, forms, and records in one place

If you don't have a designated place where you keep records and files, *make one*. It doesn't have to be an office or even a file cabinet. A set of cardboard boxes will do, if that's all you can muster. The important thing is – designate a place for your files, and gather all your files in that place. And keep them there.

Organize

Don't be intimidated by your papers and the pressure to employ the perfect filing system. There is no perfect filing system. But – there are several logical ways in which you can organize your papers, so decide what works best for you and do it. You might, for example, group all financial records in one section, in green folders; another group of files for insurance records in blue folders; another for medical records in red folders; a section for bills in yellow folders, and so on. Within each section, you can then alphabetize your files.

Maintain

Here's where many people fall down on the job and why so many filing systems fail; they are not maintained. You must take grown-up responsibility for filing papers as they come into your home, whether it be every day after the mail is sorted, or once a week or once a month. If all your papers are in one place, the filling isn't so onerous. There are two keys to making this work: 1) keep all "filing to do" papers on one place, always – say, a basket on the hall table, where you open the mail, and 2) when you file your papers, throw away any documents that are being replaced by what you're filing – toss last month's gas bill, for example, when you file this month's bill. That way, your files don't become unwieldy.

You're Not The Keeper of the Paperwork In Your Marriage?

Fine, great – it's really nice to have a partner who's willing to do all of that work. But – do insist on all files being in one place. Do insist that they are all open for inspection at all times; nothing under lock and key, unless you have your own personal copy of those keys. Do check to make sure that filing is being kept up to date. If not, then pitch in and help with the filing yourself. And finally, look in the files. Review bills and financial records regularly, and read and understand all legal documents such as the deed to your home, your living trust and powers of attorney if you have them, business ownership, asset ownership, and the like. If you don't understand any or all of the above, sit down with your spouse to discuss until you do understand – or take the documents you don't understand to your accountant, lawyer, or trusted advisor to review and explain to you.

Assets & Liabilities Inventory

Create a file all on its own in the financial section of your files, just for recording all of your assets and liabilities. In this file, list everything you own:

a. Bank accounts – banking institution, names on account, account number
b. Stocks, bonds, mutual funds, other investments – again list the institution or company, number of shares owned or nature of ownership, account number
c. Special savings accounts such as college savings accounts
d. Retirement accounts – type of account, institution where account is held, name on account, account number
e. Credit cards – institution, name(s) on account, account number
f. Mortgage, home equity account, other loans - institution, name(s) on account, account number
g. Autos – make, model, name(s) on title, VIN number
h. Other assets – boats, RVs, second homes, businesses you own or in which you've invested
i. Copy of deed to your home if you own your home
j. Valuables such as jewelry, artwork, antiques
k. Make it an ironclad rule to review and update your assets & liabilities inventory on a regular basis – quarterly, biannually, or at a minimum, annually.

Financial Management

Managing your money isn't about restricting yourself and living like a penny pincher, as many people seem to feel. It's about making your life fit your money and being able to make decisions about what you can and cannot do and can and cannot have with confidence and without undue stress and worry. Without a budget, you run the risk of either overspending – and building up debt, incurring late fees, and generally living from crisis to crisis – or underspending, and denying yourself the enjoyments of life that you can very well afford.

a. Create a Budget - This can be as ornate as an accounting spreadsheet or as simple as a hand-written list of monthly income and bills and discretionary expenses with your estimate or monthly limit listed next to each item. The bottom line: it's a plan that shows you how much you can spend, how much you have spent, and whether you're running in the black or the red. Make it a monthly practice to review the money that actually came in and went out versus your budget.

b. Create a Schedule or Calendar for Paying Your Bills – If you're not an online banking aficionado, get a simple wall calendar and write in bills that you must pay on the appropriate dates. Not only will you track monthly expenses, but you'll be sure to keep on top of quarterly and semiannual payments as well.

c. Online Banking – In this day and age, it is highly recommended that you take advantage of online banking, which gives you the greatest and most immediate control of your expenditures. With online banking you can schedule automatic bill payments, pay individual bills at any time, check your bank balances, transfer funds among accounts, stop payments, and send money to individuals. If you or your spouse have not set up online banking, do so now, and log in and check accounts frequently. And note – for all accounts that you share with your spouse, set up your *own* individual login for the account, if at all possible. (Some banks will allow login accounts only for the "primary account holder." If this is the case, be sure you have the login even if it's technically under your spouse's name. It's your account too and you're entitled to the same access he has.)

Rest & Rejuvenation

a. This may seem crazy simple, but honestly, sleep is the great power tool. No matter what else is going on in your life, get your sleep every night. Medical evidence abounds about the benefits of sleep and the harmful effects of the lack thereof. Lack of sleep reduces your ability to handle stress, problem solve, ward off illness, exercise, keep an even temper, and even control your eating.

b. Healthy escapism is a very effective reset button for your life too.

Meditation, even for five minutes a day, can give your emotions, brain, and body the chance to reboot and start fresh. Watching a comforting old sitcom for a half hour can relieve you of stress. Getting a mani pedi can make you feel pampered and calm.

c. Pay attention to your daily pace and make sure you reserve time each day, even if just a few minutes, to "step away" from it all. You may not be able to make your problems go away, but you can make their load a little lighter by making sure you have enough rest and you "check out" regularly in order to recharge.

Fresh Air & Exercise

Like sleep, fresh air and exercise are essential to good physical and mental health. You already know what the advice is about the appropriate amount of exercise for your age and circumstances, so we won't repeat all of that information here. But we do have a few pieces of advice that are particularly appropriate to women with spouses, families, or divorces looming.

a. First, don't be guilted into sacrificing your health for the sake of everyone else's schedules and needs. If you are not taking time to exercise and get outside regularly, you are literally shortening your life and compromising your health and mobility in your later years. Is that kind of sacrifice justified – by anything? Do NOT let your physical health get thrown away for the sake of others.

b. Second, if you struggle to "make" yourself go to the gym or to exercise class, how about this? Don't! Exercise is as much about feeling good and enjoying your body as it is about maintaining your weight and keeping your blood pressure down. So don't engage in exercise that you find to be drudgery. Find and enjoy activities that you, well, enjoy! It might be a dance class. It might be riding a bike without pressure to go a certain distance. It might be roller skating at a local rink. Find something you actually look forward to doing.

c. Third, be aware of the power of sabotage on the part of an uncooperative or downright hostile spouse. If you have children and you find that your husband is constantly letting you down when he promises to come home in time to let you get to an evening Pilates class or stay home on a Saturday so you can go on a bike ride, take the power of sabotage away from him. Stop factoring him into your plans, even if he should be fair and take responsibility for the kids a reasonable amount of the time. Forget it. Hire a babysitter or make arrangements with friends to swap playdates or find a facility that provides childcare for exercising moms – or whatever arrangement you can come up with.

Making Good Memories

This is more a philosophical outlook on life than a how-to, but think about this: Every day you are making memories – for yourself, for your partner, for your children. Try to make good ones, every day – and not for one or the other, but for all three – you, him, and them. Sure, there's drudgery without limit sometimes, and if you're going through a crisis, there may be many bad to terrible things going on that you cannot control, but there's something good in every day, even if it's a moment of crazy laughter at the absurdity of it all. Show yourself and especially show your children that no matter what, basically life is good, you and they are loved, and regardless of what's going on, you can always appreciate kindness or beauty or happy discoveries or just the great good fortune of loving and being loved.

CHECKLIST OF WHAT TO DO, AND WHEN, IF YOU BELIEVE (OR KNOW) THAT THE MARRIAGE IS FAILING

1. **Find a lawyer.** This is never a premature step. Whether you actually end up going through a divorce or not, every decision you make from the moment you believe your marriage is in trouble should be made with as much information and expert advice as you can gather. Get your advocate in place right now.

2. **Find a financial advisor.** You have to know what you own, what your income and expenses are, and what your financial situation is likely going to be should you divorce. An accountant and/or financial planner can help you collect all of the information you need and analyze it according to the what-if's that you're facing.

3. **Gather all of your financial records and create an inventory of all assets and liabilities.** (See the Step-By-Step Guide for a list of what you should include.) Make a copy of everything and keep those copies safe in a place only you can access.

4. **Get the best information you can regarding your husband's income** – pay stubs, bonuses he's likely to receive, tax refunds he may have coming, pension plan his employer may be contributing to, rent from properties held, return on investments, etc.

5. **Stop pooling your money with your spouse, if possible.** If you're earning an income and you've been depositing your paychecks into a joint account, stop. Open a separate account of your own and have your paychecks deposited there. Do continue to keep up your fair share of household expenses, but preserve as much of your own income as possible.

6. **Let your attorney know immediately if you believe that your spouse is hiding income or assets – or debts.**

7. **Request credit reports on yourself from all three credit reporting bureaus.** Make sure that there aren't new credit cards or loans taken out with your name on them. Notify all three bureaus that you want your credit locked down as of now; i.e., no new credit cards or loans can be taken out with your name on them.

8. **Find a person who can provide emotional support and who can be trusted to keep what you share to him or herself.** This may be a sister, best friend, counselor, clergyperson, mother, father - whomever. You do need someone to talk to. Think about who that would be, whether they have the emotional space for you, and whether they can be compassionate and fair-minded. Avoid bonding to anyone negative or bitter, especially another woman who's going through what you're going through. Chances are she will be going through her own coping and healing process and will have difficulty providing wise and unbiased counsel.

9. **Make a plan for telling your children, your friends, and anyone else who needs to know that you're going through a divorce.** Consider how your divorce may affect others and use that perspective to decide whether you should fill them in on what's going on. You may not want to share your personal life with your boss, for example, but if you know you're going to need time off for appointments with your attorney and accountant, or you're going to have to shoulder more child care responsibilities, it's best to let your boss know as early on as possible.

10. **Seek support from a counselor, clergyperson, support group, or other neutral source of encouragement, hope, and information.**

11. **Be conscientious about getting your rest and exercise.** The benefits are many. You will be stronger and better able to weather the stresses facing you, which means you'll be insuring the best outcome for yourself and your children that you possibly can.

12. **Don't let your clothing and grooming fall into disrepair.** Though you may feel that you don't know where the next penny is coming from, do keep in mind that you aren't likely to go from riches to rags. Your standard of living may fall, but that doesn't mean that you can't afford anything anymore. It's important for your self esteem and mental health to take care of your appearance. Maybe you can't go to the high-end hairdresser you've been going to for years, but don't automatically give up. Tell you hairdresser what's going on; maybe she'll give you a discount while you're going through your divorce. Or find an acceptable hairdresser who's less pricey. The same with clothes; maybe you'll have to switch from Ann Taylor to Target, but there are many respectable designers whose lines are in the less expensive stores. And, if you're really under financial constraints, there's no shame in shopping at consignment stores. Find the ones in the more upscale neighborhoods; you'll be surprised how often you can find high-quality garments that are practically new – or that even still have their tags on!

13. **Stay optimistic, and keep your sense of humor.** No really. This is a *time* in your life. It's not your *whole* life. You will get through it, there is more to come, and despite what you may feel at the moment, you're growing tremendously from this whole experience. **There's a better, stronger you evolving. Embrace it.**

For sales, editorial information, subsidiary rights information or a
catalog, please write or
phone or email:

Brick Tower Press
Manhanset House
Dering Harbor, New York 11965-0342
Sales: 1-800-68-BRICK
Tel: 212-427-7139
www.ibooksinc.com
email: bricktower@aol.com

www.IngramContent.com

CPSIA information can be obtained
at www.ICGtesting.com
Printed in the USA
LVOW05*0431230817
546051LV00005B/12/P